Bill,

You are [a]
story-telle[r]
thankful to have spent the day
with you! May God richly bless
you as you connect with others
through the written word and

the Ultimate
COMMAND

your magnetic personality!

— Tommy Bates

THOMAS C. BATES, M.S.

the Ultimate COMMAND

Relearning the Principles of Loving God, Others & Yourself

TATE PUBLISHING
AND ENTERPRISES, LLC

Published by Tate Publishing & Enterprises, LLC
127 E. Trade Center Terrace | Mustang, Oklahoma 73064 USA
1.888.361.9473 | www.tatepublishing.com

Tate Publishing is committed to excellence in the publishing industry. The company reflects the philosophy established by the founders, based on Psalm 68:11,
"The Lord gave the word and great was the company of those who published it."

Book design copyright © 2012 by Tate Publishing, LLC. All rights reserved.
Cover design by Kenna Davis
Interior design by Chelsea Womble

Published in the United States of America

ISBN: 978-1-61862-817-6
1. Religion / Christian Life / General
2. Religion / Christian Life / Love & Marriage
12.04.25

First, this book is dedicated to my precious wife, Jessica Bates, whose love, devotion, and attention to detail made this possible, and to my precious children, Jordan, Gina, Chloe, and Gabriel, who inspire me to love every day.

Second, this book is dedicated to my mother, Faye Moore, and sister, Lorri Crumpton, whose grace, compassion, and dedication to me and my family have been an inspiration.

Last, I dedicate this book to my stepmother Carol and my precious father, Larry Bates, who learned to love well. I will never forget you. I will see you again.

ACKNOWLEDGEMENTS

There are many who have crossed my path and helped shape my vision of love, showing me the way to express it. While I cannot name them all, I can mention these:

- Belle P. Faulk, my precious grandmother.
- Dr. Garner V. Clark, pastor, mentor and friend.
- Sonny Kirk, pastor, mentor.
- Kent Bailey
- Dr. Charles "Chuck" Swindoll
- Dr. Charles Stanley
- Dr. James Dobson
- Rev. Billy Graham
- My true friend, Dave Hicks.
- My best man and teacher, Ken Jones.
- Tate Publishing, who shared my vision and helped to spread the message of love.

TABLE OF CONTENTS

INTRODUCTION

In the busy lives most of us lead, few of us have time for reading, especially non-fiction. Those who are not motivated professionally are hard pressed to find time to do more than skim and speed read non-fiction works. Upon seeing the title of this book, one might see a subject that, like so many others, may seem overused. *It seems obvious that we need to love*, you might wonder. Like a person sitting through the same tithing message in church that you have heard year after year, there are many subjects about which we feel there is nothing more to learn.

The Ultimate Command, emphasizing loving God and loving others, is one of those issues we hear about in church circles, on Christian radio, and elsewhere. Perhaps that is the reason a specific book has not been written, about such an obvious tenet of the Christian faith. Is it possible we assume everyone knows the importance of love with regard to our faith?

What we need to realize is the fact that, like many other subjects about which we are jaded, we have much head knowledge but little application thereof. As I have heard many teachers say, there are roughly twelve inches between the head and the heart. And the evidence in our society would suggest among those of us who have forgotten how to love as God intended, just as many are either beaten down by life, bitter from past hurts, or too busy to practice what we believe in real life. Love is *the most* important part of being a Christian, and it is one of the basic principles of the Christian life that is paramount in becoming more like Christ. We will be judged more severely regarding how we love than any other aspect, any other element of our behavior, attitude of the heart in our Christian walk.

Many people reading this book may be experiencing doubts, confusion, and various crises in their lives. Maybe they are doubting Christianity, doubting God, or finding the Christian life to be more trouble than it is worth. I, too, have experienced doubts, even in the process of writing this book. I do not believe I have ever found myself in more dire financial or emotional stress in all my life than I have while writing this book. Our economy has plummeted, jobs are scarce, and gasoline and other fuel expenses are outrageously beyond what is reasonable.

Our family has struggled to survive, and I have found myself fighting to remain hopeful, straining to keep afloat. We have been forced to make very difficult choices, choosing between allowing utilities to be disconnected or to pay rent. We have been forced to seek local community resources wherever possible—all the while facing the continual stress of having special needs children who are in school systems with marginal resources to provide for their needs. On many occasions I have asked, "Why do you keep pressing us, God?

In the midst of our struggles, I have had very little love to offer. Our drive, our desire to follow Christ, sometimes rises and falls with the circumstances we experience. But all the while, in the midst of God's process of testing me, developing my courage, hammering me over and over with difficulties, I find myself longing for more of Him. When I am nearest to my blessed Father, that is when I feel His peace; His soothing presence washes away the anger and the bitterness and leaves me at rest. Like medicine for the soul, the Holy Spirit is ever present and ready to comfort me when I hurt.

In spite of the pain and frustration, there have been glimmers of hope, immediate answers to prayer, and gifts from strangers anonymously given to our family to keep us from going under. We hold on to these moments to get us through the difficult times, remembering how He has brought us through many times before. Though He cannot be seen, God is as real as the breath in my lungs and the electricity powering the computer on which I am typing this book. How quickly I doubt and forget all the hard times He has delivered me from previously! May God grant you strength to endure whatever you face today.

I pray this book will help you experience God's power as you fulfill the most important part of our shared faith. In focusing on loving God and striving to love others, may you find the peace that surpasses all understanding. If you focus your energy on love, on God, on sharing love with others, you will be transformed. As you turn your mind from your circumstances and toward God, may you find the peace that surpasses all understanding (Philippians 4:7). And may God, through His Holy Spirit, help you apply what you read in the pages of this book to your life, not only acknowledging the wisdom herein but being willing to make changes as God directs you.

WHY SHOULD WE LOVE?

The speaker crackles to life as John hears, "Good morning. Welcome to Joey's. May I take your order?"

"Yes, I want a small coffee and a sausage biscuit with no egg but with cheese. No *heuvos*, got that?"

The garbled reply doesn't give him much confidence that she understood him. After a curt exchange of money, then food, John speeds away. One block down the street, as he pulls out his sausage, *egg*, and cheese biscuit from the wrapper, he snaps. "That stupid woman, how many times have I gone through the drive-through and told them the same thing day after day? And day after day, they get it wrong!" He removes the poached circle-shaped egg from the biscuit, flings it out the window, and *splat*—it lands squarely on the windshield of the car behind him.

As the driver behind John aggressively begins to pass him, now staring at the newly attached ornamental egg plastered on his windshield, he realizes John has a fish emblem on his trunk. In addition, he sees the "Honk if you Love Jesus" sticker on John's bumper. As he passes John, he tries to keep himself in check and honks, watching in horror as John, *Mr. Christian*, gives him an inappropriate, one-fingered gesture.

Day after day, our world becomes more calloused. Year after year, the stories on the news show clearly the verse in Matthew that states, "...the love of most will grow cold" (Matthew 24:12). Children murdered by their parents, parents murdered by their children—the list goes on and on. Our world has grown colder. Yes, there are bright spots in places, and some still have kindness, but the large majority of us are less friendly, more impatient, and lack not only common courtesy but compassion, as well.

Impersonal, hermit-like creatures we have become, doing business online and spending hours at home. We have no semblance of the social behavior our ancestors had, partly due to the busy, chaotic lifestyles we lead, and partly from sheer laziness and selfishness with our personal time. Interacting face to face requires effort, and we have no need for it with social networking, texting, and instant messaging. We have lost the art of connection, and with it has come the decline of love for mankind. God is whispering in your ear. Are you listening? Do you hear His patient voice reminding you to open up your heart and love?

What kind of book is this? Is this is it yet another book about love? The answer is *yes*; it is a book about love. Am I asking you to become some spineless, sappy wimp who gets kicked around by the rest of the world? The answer is an emphatic *no*. Maybe you are thinking, "I'm just not that type of person. I say what I mean and mean what I say, and I'm not about to change." The ultimate love does not require backing down from that which you passionately defend or are convinced of, and

God will never ask you to be a wimp. The greatest love is true love, biblical love, the kind of love that is commanded by scripture. Real love requires guts, intentionally caring for others enough to confront them, graduating from selfishness and emotional immaturity, and reaching out to one another.

Maybe you have been hurt. Maybe you have become hardened by the critical nature of a parent, spouse, or ex-spouse, co-workers, the community with whom you relate, or the friends with whom you surrounded yourself. Maybe cynicism, disconnection from others, is a part of your culture or upbringing. Whether you are a realist, an Atheist, Agnostic, Catholic, Protestant, Evangelical, or a member of any other world religion, you are missing one of life's greatest pleasures if you do not love.

Have you heard of Abraham Maslow? One of the most fascinating concepts I ever learned in my first psychology class more than twenty years ago was Maslow's hierarchy of needs. This psychologist framed his theory with a pyramid that included a hierarchy of the most basic needs at the bottom to the highest need for self-actualization at the top. (Maslow 1970).[1]

Let's examine a hypothetical high-school student, whom we will call Joe and who has just finished his senior year. Let's say his parents have had enough of his free-loading, partying, and running wild. They sit him down, quietly, and explain to him the value of living on his own. "Okay, Joe, you've lived with us for eighteen years. Now it's time for you to strike out on your own."

Headstrong and feeling as though he has the world by the tail, Joe agrees and decides, "Okay, I'm ready."

Joe's parents give him his graduation money and give him a couple of weeks to find an apartment, and off he goes. Well, Joe has some very important decisions to make. He finds an apartment and thinks, *I'll have to pay rent, deposit, utilities, water, cable TV ... and I might want to eat,* so he looks for and secures a job at a local fast food restaurant. Joe is focused on the first two needs described by Maslow—first, physiological needs like food and shelter for today, and, second, safety and security needs like food and shelter for tomorrow, employment that will ensure a consistent paycheck for next month's bills, and so forth.

Now, pretty soon, Joe gets lonely in his little apartment and says to himself, "I need to have a girlfriend." At this point, Joe has moved higher on the pyramid to the third level, seeking belongingness and love. Joe connects with a girlfriend and is smart enough to have a friend move in to help pay the bills. Even still, he starts wondering if flipping burgers is "the life" for him. His bills are barely getting paid, and he's finding it hard to have enough left over to take his girlfriend out to the movies. "Maybe I should think about getting a better job," Joe muses. Joe has now moved up to the fourth level of the pyramid—esteem needs, or the need for achievement, status, self-esteem, and confidence.

Upon knocking on several doors and filling out several applications, Joe says to himself, "I really need to find something I enjoy—something I'm gifted at, and I will get the training I need to get into that field." Joe is finally moving toward the fifth and highest level of the pyramid, which is finding self-actualization.

THOMAS C. BATES, M.S.

What in the world is self-actualization? In plain English, it means to fulfill one's potential completely, achieve complete personal growth, and feel satisfied. While this is a simple definition, accomplishing it may be very complicated, indeed. I might point to my own life whereby I changed college majors five times and worked in over twenty jobs in less than twenty years, including driving a flatbed eighteen-wheeler over the road, elevator construction, data entry, teaching junior high and high school mathematics, and working in a research and development lab, to name a few. I digress.

To achieve complete happiness—to live in such a way that in reaching the end, you feel a sense of accomplishment—that is a life truly blessed. How do we get there? Ultimately, I believe giving of yourself, positively affecting others and leaving an impact on those you encounter is a worthy pursuit. Loving others, the outward expression of love to those with whom you connect is, in itself, the greatest way to live. Love encourages, enhances, builds bridges, and leaves a positive impact upon those who receive it. Love leaves things better than they were before you touched them; it is the most transcendent, honorable way to live. One who endeavors to love will never regret the decision to do so. It is a most worthy pursuit that, in itself, brings contentment and joy.

Self-actualization is a term that makes sense to most people. I must explain, however, that I do not believe actualization is complete when it depends upon the "self" to accomplish it. While many find meaning in their lives through their employment and their calling in life and achieve some measure of peace and contentment in doing what they feel they are meant to do with their lives, I must ask the reader a few pertinent, however common, questions. Why are you here? For what purpose were you born? What is this human race all about, and what were we made to do?

I do not claim to have all the answers, but everyone should, at some point, take a step back from their busy lives and ponder these questions. Are we here by chance? Did we evolve from a primal sludge that resulted from a huge explosion in the sky? I am neither a philosopher nor a scientist and will not take the time to make an argument other than to call your attention to this simple but poignant point. The complexities of the human organs, the eye, the heart, the brain, the delicate balance that exists in our planet's distance from the sun, gravity; the list goes on and on, all these fascinating and complex aspects of our world are too amazing to me to have evolved from a simple explosion in the universe.

To you who disagree with intelligent design, I simply request that you be objective as I have always tried to be and be willing to open your mind to the possibility that your professors may have been wrong. To you, I say to open the Bible with an objective, critical mind and try to disprove it as so many others have. As Isaiah put it, "Come, let us reason together, says the Lord" (Isaiah 1:18). There are many scholarly, educated individuals who set their minds and hearts to disprove the scriptures only to fall at the feet of the king of the universe and realize their need for Him. That is my challenge to you: read the Bible for yourself and remain objective, if only to indulge your curiosity. What do you have to lose?

Having stated my belief in intelligent design, I must conclude, then, that there is a designer. Since there is but one book that has stood the test of time and explains the origin of species, the age of the Earth, and the order in it, I must also conclude that the Bible is the source of truth from which I can derive explanations for my questions. Not merely questions about my origin and existence, but also questions about my purpose, the purpose of the human race, how to find fulfillment and many others. I could argue about the existence of absolute truth versus post-modern thought, but I will limit my discussion to one simple precedent: absolute truth exists. It exists in a person, and that person is Jesus Christ. He is the fulfillment of all three hundred plus prophecies about himself, in significant detail, the odds of which seem impossible to calculate. For example, Professor Peter Stoner, the chairman of mathematics and astronomy at Pasadena City College in 1944 calculated that the odds of one person fulfilling forty eight of the more than three hundred prophecies of the Christ were ten to the one hundred fifty-seventh power (Stoner 2002).[2] My conclusion is that Jesus exists, was and is the Messiah, was born of a virgin, died for my failures so I could justifiably enter heaven, and rose from the dead just as was predicted thousands of years before He was born on the earth.

Morality exists, conscience exists, and truth exists. Yes, some ignore their conscience, and in doing so may become calloused and indifferent, but the truth exists whether one believes it or not. Laws and values exist for a reason. They keep us from chaos and provide order.

Having laid a foundation for truth, I contend further that if Jesus is the Christ, and the scripture is God's legacy for believers' meditation, actions, and conformation to the likeness of Christ, then the words Christ spoke are of special importance. If Christ is the King of kings and the Lord of lords, would you not agree with me that the words He chose to speak in his thirty-three years upon this earth are worthy of exceptional contemplation? The ultimate command comes from the gospel of Matthew. Jesus had just finished defending himself against the Sadducees, a religious group who believed there was no resurrection and wanted to trick Him into perjuring Himself. Another religious group, the legalistic Pharisees, had one of their experts ask Him a question with the same motive.

> "'Teacher, which is the greatest commandment in the Law?' Jesus replied: "'Love the Lord your God with all your heart and with all your soul and with all your mind." This is the first and greatest commandment. And the second is like it: "Love your neighbor as yourself."' All the Law and the Prophets hang on these two commandments" (Matthew 22:36-40).

What a statement! Could anything be more important? Every person, every church, and every Christian entity that binds itself to the Holy Scripture should take note. This is our calling! Great or small, every living creature that calls himself a Christian, every organization, every non-profit business, everyone everywhere, should have this scripture as its creed. It is the heart of everything and should be the focus, the central hub, and the driving force behind everything that is done for the kingdom of God. Are you listening? *Nothing*, again I say, *nothing* is more important.

This book is built upon the foundation of this scripture. If you consider your existence, if you wonder why you are on the earth, if you seek fulfillment or "self-actualization," then look no further! If you believe in God and His son Jesus Christ, then you *must* consider this verse. Jesus said "All the Law and the Prophets hang on these two commands." That means the whole book, the whole scripture, everything rests on this premise. That is why it is the ultimate command. To those of you who seek, who may not believe as of yet, I offer this scripture as a building block to a faith I pray you embrace. Nothing is more important than loving God and loving others. Many churches, like the temple in which Jesus drove out the money lenders, have lost sight of its purpose. Many organizations and many believers have moved away from this simple but life-altering command.

We engage in the business of the church, sometimes becoming mired down with committees, and we lose ourselves in the busy-*ness* of life. But every one of us needs to get back to this simple command. I am certainly not stating that the business of church is evil, or that committees, activities, witnessing, events, concerts, sermons, jobs, fund-raisers, or any endeavor within the church is necessarily evil. But what is the motive behind it? What is our purpose as a church? As individuals?

Regardless of their lifestyle or their hang-ups, the way they dress or smell, whether pierced or tattooed, whether dying of AIDS, addiction, or a homosexual lifestyle, whether successful and promising or sleeping on the streets, everyone around us needs love. Did I say it is merely a good idea or a good suggestion to love others? I did not! You and I are *commanded* to do it every day, whether we feel like it or not.

God created us to love and glorify Him—to bring Him honor. Our very beings resonate with this. As humans, we cry out to belong to another to fellowship with another. Yes, there are exceptions; some people are just not "people persons," but that is not what God intended. If they search themselves, individuals who do not want to interact with others frequently are that way because they have been hurt. Either they have been wounded deeply by others, have something to hide, or they suffer from some type of emotional or mental deficit, dysfunction, or disorder.

God created us to inter-relate, to commune with Him, and to relate to others. "As iron sharpens iron, so one man [or woman] sharpens another" (Proverbs 27:17). Some people have been hurt or conditioned to turn away from others. That is neither God's intent nor doing, but rather the sinful world and its effects that have created such persons. Some have been turned off from church through bad experiences or through being burned by other believers who still have a sinful nature and, therefore, still make mistakes. Some are turned off by the business of the church or the traditionalism that narrowly sets itself against the world so strongly that as the late Christian comedian Jerry Clower put it, "They've become so heavenly minded, they are no earthly good."

As the historian Jaroslav Pelikan put it, "Tradition is the living faith of the dead, traditionalism is the dead faith of the living." Those bound by traditionalism have forgotten Paul's words when he said, "I have become all things to all people, so that by all means possible I might win others to the Lord" (1 Corinthians 9:22). But whatever your reason for avoiding fellowship with others, you are missing out on part of the ultimate command—loving others as yourself.

God has called you to relate to Himself first and then to others, and to do so with love as your motive. There is no higher purpose. Everything an individual or the church does should filter through this verse to ensure that love is at its core, and that every activity is purposed in love. You might say, "I clean toilets for a living," or "I kill roaches for a living. Am I supposed to do this in love?" and the answer is *yes*. We are to love every person with whom we come into contact whether it is face-to-face or over the phone. "Even the boss who berates me in front of others?" you may counter. Yes, especially him. That is our calling—every day of our lives. Young and old, male and female, parents and children, all of us share this purpose. Ask yourself, am I living up to this mission and this purpose? Pray with me to make this your life's work.

WHAT IS LOVE?

Love is a complex, multi-faceted term that can apply to people, animals, even objects. As such, the concept of love is hard to define in a broad sense. A person might love her cat, another his car, and both may love their spouses at the same time. The ancient Greeks, in creating their language, were able to differentiate between the various types of love by using unique words for each. For example, the Greek term *storge* represents affection due to familiarity—love toward family that does not necessarily depend upon the other person doing something to deserve love, such as a mother loving an infant child. While the child, however precious and sweet, may have done nothing but lie there and require constant care, a typical mother will love that child immensely.

Brotherly love, or the love for friends, family, and community, in the Greek language is *philia*. This word refers to love that is not erotic in nature. *Eros* is the Greek word for passionate love, it can mean sexual love but may also be used to describe the non-sexual attraction that exists between lovers—a love that is deeper than *philia*. *Agape* love denotes deep respect for another, and in biblical language suggests self-sacrificing love, love that is transcendent and above any other love.

Agape love, in the biblical sense, should be expressed by believers toward God first and then toward all others, whether friend or foe. *Agape* will be referred to throughout this book as the type of love commanded by scripture. *Agape* love encompasses all of the other attributes of *storge*, *philia*, and the non-sexual passionate *eros*, but is transcendent and thereby exceeds the first three types of love.

Love is affection; love is tender feelings and emotion, but its expression can vary greatly depending upon the maturity level of the person who is expressing it. For example, most everyone has experienced and most likely witnessed another in the throes of "puppy love," when a young person grows fond of a member of the opposite sex for the first time. To the boy or girl feeling those emotions, every fiber of their being feels as though it is experiencing love, and as far as the young person is concerned, they are in love. What proceeds is often an almost comical exchange—shyness and embarrassment whenever asked about their feelings or whenever an adult mentions the relationship. Notes are often passed between them with the inevitable question, "Do you like me? Check 'yes' or 'no.'" Maybe they talk on the phone, or perhaps only see each other in social settings like school or church. Then, after a couple of weeks, sometimes only days, they decide to break up, and their whirlwind romance is over almost as soon as it started.

Teenagers may move on to high school and have deeper relationships. I remember counseling a young lady in junior high who actually dated a young man for over a year, which is uncommon in my experiences with younger teens. Needless to say, the break-up was devastating for her. While teenagers have a little better grasp on relationships, most, probably to their benefit, are still unable to experience love for the opposite sex that is at its deepest level. I say "to their benefit" because they are rarely ready for that type of relationship. Becoming deeply involved would not only inhibit their ability to be open to a variety of different people from which to choose a mate, but in the event of a break-up would also likely create deeper pain, like the example mentioned above. Yes, there are exceptions to this rule, and there are relationships that begin in junior high and have lasted many years. But in the present culture, especially in America, the vast majority of teenagers, particularly those sixteen and under, are not emotionally mature enough to understand mature romantic love and, therefore, are ill-prepared for a long-term relationship, especially that of marriage.

An adolescent's version of love is often only infatuation, as is the case in many teenage and sometimes even adult relationships. The person experiencing love, though immature, is loving another whether or not they understand it completely. To the lover, they are loving the only way they know how, and they will continue to do so until education through life, pain, loss, and more importantly, as the spirit of Christ teaches them a better way. How many young people have entered into marriage while infatuated with another, only to find that upon living with them for a few years, the blinders are removed, and they see the real person, with all their warts, filthy habits, selfish behavior, and/or immaturity, is revealed.

The point here is that everyone loves, and most do so sincerely to the best of their ability. But the depth of their love, the purity of it, their ability to express it completely, adequately, and wisely, depends upon their maturity level.

In Corinthians, Paul said,

> "When I was a child, I talked like a child, I thought like a child, I reasoned like a child. When I became a man, I put childish ways behind me. Now we see but a poor reflection as in a mirror; then we shall see face to face. Now I know in part; then I shall know fully, even as I am fully known" (1 Corinthians 13: 11-12).

Love is best expressed when the person doing the loving is rich in not only the knowledge of Christ but the wisdom or application thereof. One is much more equipped to engage in a loving relationship with another when one not only understands Christ's teachings about love but is able to put them into practice fully. Yes, child-like faith is valuable, even necessary, in order to experience God at His fullest; however, deep relationships like marriage require mature love which stands the test of time.

"I am a human being prone to mistakes. When will I ever be able to love another fully?" you might ask. While I certainly agree that none of us is perfect, all of us could benefit by carefully pursuing biblical wisdom before involving ourselves in loving relationships. Wherever we are on the continuum of biblical wisdom with regard to love, all of us could stand to move a little closer to Christ, and in doing so, our divorce rates, would decrease accordingly.

Love is emotion, but love is also action. True love behaves in a way that is unselfish, putting another before oneself and doing so consistently. How is that for a test of true love? How many relationships have ended painfully as a result of selfishness? To anyone who pre-scribes to the theory that children are a blank slate and only learn bad behaviors from the world around them, I ask you one question. What is one of the first words a child utters besides "mama" and "daddy?" I will bet you can guess—"Mine!" We are born selfish, and that is an attribute that I believe God has spent forty plus years hammering out of me. Is He finished? Certainly not. But I believe people can grow, and parenthood is one of the best teachers with regard to selfishness.

Given the fact that I am helping raise two autistic children, God has definitely given me much oppor-tunity to learn about my own selfishness. The strug-gle in my heart continues fiercely, but I am growing. One must be careful, however, to balance this notion of "others first" with maintaining healthy boundaries. By "boundaries" I mean knowing where "I" stops and "you" starts, avoiding people-pleasing behaviors in which one person feels compelled to make another happy, feel-ing devastated when one encounters confrontation, or feeling sadness when someone else is displeased. We will address boundaries in detail in a later chapter—particularly why love sometimes means saying no and learning to do so without fear and trembling.

HOW DOES GOD SPELL LOVE?
O-B-E-D-I-E-N-C-E

"I wish you would do your chores without me asking you to, not because you have to, but because you love me!"

Most parents, like me, have struggled with teaching their children to be obedient. While there are children who just seem compliant from birth, many are strong-willed, stubborn, and unyielding and test us to the core. But if we are honest with ourselves, we would admit that we, too, are the obstinate children, testing our heavenly Father daily when it comes to being obedient. God desires obedience more than sacrifice, more than gifts, and more than anything else. If we love Him, we will do what He says (John 14:15).

The apostle John said, "We know that we have come to know Him if we obey His commands" (1 John 2:3). Later, John said, "This is love for God: to obey His commands, and His commands are not burdensome" (1 John 5:3). When one of my children spontaneously comes to me and says, "I love you, Dad," it makes me feel warm inside and brings me great joy. When my children take out the trash without being asked or remind me that they cleaned the litter box, now, *that* is something to behold! On the one hand, I enjoy hearing them say they love me, but when they obey me, it *proves* their love. In the New Testament, James said, "But someone will say, 'You have faith; I have deeds.' Show me your faith without deeds, and I will show you my faith by what I do" (James 2:18). While God inhabits praise, and we are certainly called to praise Him throughout the Psalms and elsewhere in the Bible, the evidence of our love is in our behavior— what we do (Palms 22:3). Yes, praise Him, give Him the honor due His holy name, but show it by desiring holiness, pursuing righteousness, and becoming like Christ.

What kind of love does God require? Are we condemned if we disobey Him? Many people struggle with this issue of eternal security, whether or not we can lose our salvation. Some believe there is no validity to the "deathbed confession" whereby one who has lived a life apart from God can successfully be converted to Christianity and can go to heaven. Others believe that, upon becoming a Christian, we can fall away from God and be denied entry to heaven. Still others believe that one can lose the "gift of the Holy Spirit." While they may not lose salvation, they may temporarily lose the closeness of God's spirit inside them.

I am constantly amazed by the variety of ways in which different people interpret the wisdom of the scripture. My Bible tells me that once we become a true Christian, no one can snatch us from God's hand (John 10:28). I believe there are two different judgments that people will encounter after death. Those who have never truly become Christians will experience the great white throne judgment, in which they will be condemned to eternal separation from God in hell. The other judgment is the judgment seat of Christ, in which those who are true believers will have their works judged and will be rewarded for the good they have done while alive on this earth. God will judge Christians based upon their willingness to obey Him, to live according to the scriptures, to love Him, and to love one another.

How do we know there is eternal security for believers? Doesn't it make sense that if we disobey God, if we fail, we aren't real believers? If God requires us to be holy, even as He is holy, how can we know we cannot lose our salvation? When I answer this question, among scriptures that confirm the limitless security we have with God, I look also at the relationship we have with Him and the nature of His character. Why did God create us? God made mankind to glorify and worship Him. Imagine a kingdom in which the ruler required his subjects to love him, to bow down to him, and to revere him in all they did. If those whom he ruled did not bow or were guilty of not loving him, he sentenced them to a very cruel and horrible death. Would the love of his subjects be genuine? Would subjects love him just because they feared death? What kind of love would that be? If my wife or my children loved me because they wanted to do the honorable thing, to fulfill their duty as a wife or as a child, would that be love or involuntary servitude?

God gives us free will. He gives us the ability to think, behave, and relate to Him and to others as we choose. Our obedience is voluntary, as it should be, and it is the measure of our love for Him—if it is done with love as its motive. Just as a husband or wife longs for the love of their spouse or as parents long for their children to love them and obey them, God desires and deserves the love and devotion of His children. If we loved Him only because we were afraid of losing our salvation, our ticket to heaven, what kind of love and what kind of devotion would that be? That is not love; it is mandatory slavery.

Does this mean God is not serious about sin? Of course not. God hates sin. He hates pride, selfishness, jealousy, murder, slander, indulgence, and lies. He longs for us to be holy, to pursue purity, and to be obedient to Him. But He leaves those actions and pursuits to us that we might do so voluntarily out of gratitude for all He has done for us.

How do we know if we are believers? John said, "Everyone who believes that Jesus is the Christ is born of God" (1 John 5:1). Earlier in 1 John it says,

> "Dear children, let us not love with words or tongue but with actions and in truth. This then is how we know that we belong to the truth, and how we set our hearts at rest in His presence whenever our hearts condemn us" (1 John 3:18).

We know we belong to the truth by our love, not only love in our hearts but, more importantly, by what we do. Love requires action—reaching out, helping one another— tangible expressions of love. We prove our love by our behavior, first in behaving obediently toward God and then in behaving compassionately toward the people we encounter daily.

When it comes to loving others, measuring the impact of your life upon those around you, where do you stand? Have you purposed in your heart to make a difference, to obediently serve God by being His ambassador on earth? When you stand before God and your deeds, your life is judged by God, what will He say about how you spent your time? Did you spend every day, encounter every person with the intent of moving them forward toward Christ, teaching the world how to love sacrificially? It is not some mystical secret—loving God and others—it is a mindset. We must constantly remind ourselves, as Christians, as human beings who are part of this greater plan, we are charged with the duty to engage, build relationships, and impact others. I honestly believe of all the aspects of being a Christian, we forget our duty to love the most.

Obedience is critical to enjoying a healthy Christian life. Without it, we not only experience the consequences of disobedience but often also miss out on God's best for our lives. While God can use every failure, everything we do, for His glory, then what opportunities have we forfeited by the inappropriate choices made in life? There is a law at work—a law of sowing and reaping. God's Word spells out that He frustrates the wicked and humbles the proud. "There is a way that seems right to man, but the end thereof is destruction" (Proverbs 14:12).

"But I have heard so many preachers say we cannot be righteous or obey God on our own. It is impossible." You are absolutely right when you say you cannot obey God alone. It *is* impossible. On a good day, we might have righteous thoughts and even do some good things, but what about the other 364 days in the year? God never intended for us to be alone in this struggle for obedience. He is with us always and promises to never leave or forsake us (Deuteronomy 31:6). His Holy Spirit is with us, and we are meant to keep in step with His Spirit (Galatians 5:25). This symbiotic relationship is the means by which God intends for us to operate on a daily basis. It is in those moments when we step out of sync with the Holy Spirit and operate from the flesh that we choose to transgress God.

Obedience is the antithesis of rebellion, the opposite of sin, and it is the cornerstone of pleasing God. While, thankfully, we have been declared righteous by the blood of Christ, we are still in a position to do what we can to obey God. In the Old Testament, Samuel says, "To obey is better than sacrifice, and to heed is better than the fat of rams" (1 Samuel 15:22). To heed is to listen, pay attention to, as well as obey another. God has called us to listen to and obey Him. It is our living sacrifice to Him (Romans 12:1).

Obedience, along with submission to God, is part of the formula for overcoming sin in our lives. James explains the steps involved in overcoming evil. "Submit yourselves, then, to God. Resist the devil, and he will flee from you" (James 4:7). Submit to God; resist the devil. May that sink into our collective brains and be there on a moment-to-moment basis as the enemy launches his surprise attacks on us.

Therein lies the problem, however, as our flesh battles with our spirit. Submitting to God sounds very easy at the moment. It sounds so attainable while we are at our leisure, reading. Unfortunately, though, at a moment's notice, temptation strikes. Like the water skier's rope being pulled tight again after the boat has slowed down, we find ourselves yanked along by our emotions when we are faced with the seductive, magnetic pull of sin. Like a person raised in a big city, constantly watching their back for potential conflict, here is where we often find ourselves. No, God has not called us to be afraid but rather to be alert, sober-minded, and ready for action (1 Peter 5:8). We must find the balance between being so hyper-vigilant that we are distracted in our daily lives and preventing ourselves from being lulled to sleep and susceptible to invasion.

How do we say no to our natural desires? How do we become obedient? Why is it that some seem capable of operating within the rules and boundaries while others seem destined to struggle with all forms of addictions and compulsions? While His children have particular God-given gifts, we also have specific areas of weakness and vulnerabilities. The most terrible part of this struggle is the fact that the enemy knows us personally—knows where to hit us the hardest. If we know the areas in which we are weak, we can prepare and protect ourselves.

The secret to protection from the enemy is found in Ephesians 6, in putting on the armor of God. We keep in step with the spirit of God when we are prepared. We are equipped for battle when we have the necessary spiritual protection, and this should be a routine (not merely a ritual) we go through on a daily basis. A great teacher, Dr. Charles Stanley, once said, "I put on my spiritual armor every day before my feet hit the floor." He explained that he spent time in prayer, going through the tools described in Ephesians 6 before he even got out of bed. What a wonderful idea! Before we have a chance to sin, at the beginning of the day we can get in step with God's spirit. Then, throughout the day, we can spend time with God in prayer, even if only for a few moments, and we will be more readily prepared and less vulnerable to our enemy.

Obedience to God is easier to achieve when we are disciplined, focused in a specific direction, and have our lives in order. Most of us are so busy trying to survive, to meet all of the emotional and financial responsibilities of life—work, relationships, and parenting—we have no idea where we are going. In spite of these demands upon our time and energy, we need to take time for solitude, for reflection, and to seek direction, purpose in our lives. One of the greatest strategies of our enemy is to keep us in a constant state of busy, rigid routines. When we cannot see the forest for the trees, when we are so harried and strung out that we cannot focus, we run in circles spiritually and lose our ability to make a difference.

Haphazard living, life without vision, lends itself to vulnerability to sin, not to mention exhaustion and burnout. It is a true statement that "an idle mind is the devil's workshop." But a life that is spent while stuck in fast forward whizzes by and is gone before we have accomplished what matters most. We certainly do perish without a vision. While it may seem important, even honorable to have your child practicing soccer three times a week, going to drama twice per week, and on the math team as well, you may be overworking your child and yourself. Some choices may seem right, but cause you to be out of sync, out of balance, and lose sight of the greater objective. One important tool in staying focused and balanced is creating a mission statement for your life or your family and developing goals and priorities to help you maintain balance. Once you have created a mission statement and goals, you need discipline to redirect yourself, make decisions in light of the greater objective, and avoid sacrificing God's best for what seems to be good at the time.

Chapter thirteen deals with discipline, and there are many disciplines that can help one live a healthier, more obedient life. Accountability to another Christian believer of the same sex and regular fellowship in a healthy church, together with the disciplines of prayer, fasting, scripture memory, study, and meditation, can help believers achieve victory over sin.

There is a Native American story that describes inner struggles, similar to that of the Holy Spirit warring against the human nature. In this story, there is a good wolf and a bad wolf fighting against each other. The wolf that wins is the one you feed the most. Our spiritual lives are much like that. We must continually feed the spiritual side, focus on prayer, the spiritual disciplines, and keep fighting. When we fail, we must get up, dust ourselves off, and keep fighting no matter how often we get knocked down by failure and sin. This struggle will continue until we enter heaven, but we are charged with the duty to keep up the good fight until it is over.

Above all, we must check ourselves daily to ensure we are obedient with regard to love. Obedience for the sake of legalism, an attempt to earn our way to heaven is not God's highest calling. If we truly want to please God, we must obey Him from an inner desire to express our love to Him, not satisfy some duty or list of rules. In the same way, love should govern how we interact with others. True obedience to God includes changing how we relate, the purpose behind our connection to our fellow man. Are you willing to be obedient to God? Then you must not only strive to lovingly obey God but engage in a continual struggle with yourself to improve how you behave with others.

DEFENDING WHAT WE LOVE

Most of us have struggled with finding the balance between tolerance and having convictions, especially Christians. While many believers have a black and white perspective with regard to major moral and ethical issues—abortion, creation versus evolution, homosexuality, euthanasia, and others—many dare not talk about it in social circles for fear of rocking the boat. While we believe certain things, have a particular world view, and have drawn clear lines between what we believe to be right and wrong, at times we take a back seat when issues are discussed because we are afraid. A variety of fears often keep us from taking a stand. We fear we will not be able to give a strong enough argument; we fear confrontation or parting ways with someone close to us; we fear being held accountable for standing up as a Christian; or, worst of all, we fear being labeled as a "right wing freak" or a "Bible thumper."

It is true that God has called us to be at peace with everyone and, like Paul, become "all things to all people, so by all means we might win some" (1 Corinthians 9:22). At the same time, we are called to be prepared in season and out of season to give an answer for the hope that we have (1 Peter 3:15). There are times when we feel like loving others, and other times when we are struggling to even respond. However, God wants our lives to exude His grace, His mercy, His goodness whether we feel good or not. It should be a part of who we are and should not depend upon our mood or the circumstances we face.

"Oh," many say, "I'm not a good speaker, and I would do more harm than good by speaking up." While many of us may feel we are not effective speakers, we must take a stand. Christ said, "If anyone is ashamed of me and my words… the son of Man will be ashamed of him…" (Luke 9:26). All the believers who have a biblical world view must rise up, take a stand and do something to acknowledge publicly what they believe. If we pulled together and accomplished this, the world would not only be a better place, but the rights of Christians and other moral people would cease to be trampled upon. Do you realize the gravity of the situation with regard to your rights as a believer? I challenge you to take a look around you and see the persecution—the fact that we are losing our right not only to believe but to say so more and more every day.

Love calls us to reach out to others and to behave in a loving manner to people around us. But love does not mean cowering in a corner, becoming a punching bag, and allowing the world to tread on our rights. This nation was founded by a group of people who believed in human rights. They wanted a nation that could govern itself and be free to worship God, and they fought for inalienable rights. In other words, rights that were protected by law and could not be taken away.

Why is it then that the very faith upon which this nation was founded is the only one denied the right to speak, to be acknowledged publicly, and to thrive? As the great Irish/British spokesman Edmund Burke stated, "All that is necessary for evil to triumph is for good men to do nothing." That is the problem that faces Christianity and Christian rights. Too many are closet believers, unwilling to take a stand. There is a growing population in society today that has taken a liberal worldview and, while calling themselves Christians, stand on the side of tolerance rather than risk being labeled Conservative. "Judge not, lest ye be judged," you will often hear them say.

While I agree with the fact that scripture calls us to avoid standing in judgment, we should not take that scripture out of context, sacrifice holiness, and nullify the whole counsel of the Bible. While we are called to "avoid foolish arguments and genealogies about the law, for they are unprofitable and useless," we should not take up sides with the enemy of the Bible by sacrificing holiness and truth (Titus 3:9). Loving others does not mean fearfully turning your back on what you know to be right, for the sake of making peace. Loving God and loving others does not include omitting the principles of scripture for the sake of conformity, fitting in, or avoiding uncomfortable confrontation.

I believe this is where many have gone wrong in taking a liberal world view and is the point at which such a large group of people have stumbled. One simple question is appropriate here. Do you believe the whole counsel of God? Do you believe the whole Bible, or do you only believe part of it is true? Timothy said that *all* scripture is God-breathed and is useful for teaching, rebuking, correcting, and training in righteousness, not just the parts which make us feel warm and fuzzy (2 Timothy 3:16). If you believe scripture, then you must read about heaven and hell, the parts which explain how to get to heaven and the actions and behavior which determine that destiny. Yes, some scripture applies to a particular culture at a particular time, but if you look at the context, all of it applies. Are we to be so rigid and so legalistic that we forget the most important concept of Christianity—love? Absolutely not. But as a society we need to realize evil is triumphing every day.

Until we take a stand, vote, write our congressmen and representatives, and find ways of making a difference, we will continue to see our rights trampled upon by the enemy. I pray for our nation and the world that we will unite as Christians and lovingly confront post-modernism, tolerance, and the subtle attack from the enemy of our souls. Find the time to do something once a week or once a month that lovingly confronts that which you believe to be contrary to your faith.

But do not forget that the method in which you confront, the attitude of your heart, should still reflect the love of Christ. The fruit of the Spirit should be evident in your heart while you relate to everyone, even those in opposition to you. We need to find a healthy balance between running from conflict, hiding inside our comfort zones, and avoiding leaving a bad taste in the mouths of those we confront. The next chapter of this book deals with how to lovingly confront those with whom you disagree.

THOMAS C. BATES, M.S.

LOVING CONFRONTATION

One of the most difficult concepts of the Christian life, one that I believe is a major problem in the church and in everyday relationships, is that of loving confrontation. In society today, much has been said in the way of tolerance. Most are afraid to confront evil and are afraid to ruffle feathers—afraid to say what needs to be said. On the other hand, others seem to thrive upon conflict and appear to not only lack empathy and compassion but also the slightest bit of concern for others' feelings.

There is a balance between standing up for what one believes and running roughshod over people. Yes, sometimes Christ is offensive to others, and swimming against the tide of humanity stirs up anger. But we are commanded in scripture to live in peace with one another as it pertains to us, and we need to choose our battles carefully, doing so with grace, compassion, and the gentleness of the spirit of Christ, speaking and behaving in a way that reflects Christ's love and sacrifice. Without compassion and without mercy, what kind of Christ are others seeing?

Confrontation is a very delicate matter and should be done only after careful consideration. Our goal should be to build a relationship rather than tear it down. If you lack compassion for the person you want to confront, pray for God's grace to help you see through their eyes. If you cannot, then do the body of Christ a favor and leave room for the Holy Spirit to do His work. In other words, if you cannot do it with genuine compassion and with the intention of building a relationship, building a bridge between Christ and another, then I suggest avoiding or postponing confronting this person.

When you are faced with a situation where confrontation is necessary and appropriate, find a suitable setting, and a good time when you will be able to speak to the person or persons. Take them out to lunch or meet them in their home—a place where you will feel comfortable having an uninterrupted conversation. Biblical confrontation calls for taking one or more witnesses with you, people who share the burden for this person. Fellow believers who accompany you in this situation should share your desire to restore the one whom you are confronting if at all possible. If you are able, take some time to write down the issues you want to discuss beforehand; you may even want to keep them at hand during the conversation in case your emotions get in the way. Be careful not to use words like "you," "always," or "never" and keep the emphasis on yourself rather than pointing blame. Placing the emphasis on yourself helps avoid causing the person you are confronting to put up walls and become defensive. Use words that describe your feelings. "When you do this, it makes me feel _____." Another person cannot argue with how you feel. Yes, you may feel uncomfortable, especially when you begin this process, but think of the result and think of the release—the burden being lifted from finally initiating change.

When you have finished the confrontational situation, whether a small situation at work or a heartfelt discussion you have with someone after years of holding in your feelings, review it in your mind. Did you think through your response? Did you consider all options and present it in a peaceable way to the best of your ability? Once you have weighed all that you said, decided that this is the best way, and that you were within your rights and it was appropriate to say it, relax. If there are points at which you feel you failed, if you feel as though you allowed your emotions to cause you to be hurtful, then find an opportunity to apologize. Always, whether you feel the person deserves it or not, has repented or continues to fail, you must do what you can to be at peace and encourage restoration. You are not responsible for their behavior, their recovery, or their growth but rather how you responded, how you reacted, and your actions.

Once you have prepared what you need to say to whomever needs to be confronted and you have said what needs to be said in the nicest way you can, then you need to let that be the end of it. No more taking responsibility for others' feelings. How they respond to what you have said is their business. And by all means, open the door for the relationship as soon as you are able, however uncomfortable it may be. Reconciliation means that to the best of your ability you are willing to maintain the relationship. Only in the most difficult situations, where you feel you cannot relate to another without constantly being wounded or when some behavior in which they engage violates your conscience should you intentionally remove yourself from the relationship. To relate to another in love means you are willing to do the best to maintain peace so far as it depends upon you (Hebrews 12:14).

Finally, we as Christians need to admonish one another, to urge one another on toward good character. God has called us to teach and help each other learn what is right. In this age of tolerance, there is a place for confrontation. Love does not mean we merely gloss over issues that are worthy of our concern. There are important moments when we need to speak up.

We ourselves need to be teachable, flexible, and willing and open to others. Without teachable spirits, we stagnate and become useless for the kingdom of heaven. We must be like David who said, "Let a righteous man strike me—it is a kindness; let him rebuke me—it is oil on my head. My head will not refuse it" (Psalms 141:5). With thick enough skin to endure persecution and soft enough hearts to accept God's gentle urgings, we will remain true to the calling of God in our lives. As difficult as it is for some, challenging, teaching, and even rebuking others is sometimes exactly what another needs to hear. All the while, however, we must remember to communicate love, our desire to help in the process. Be willing and be obedient, no matter the cost, to patiently serve God with not only the easy but the difficult tasks, as well. May God bless you richly as you persevere, grow through conflict and stand firm for the faith.

WE WORSHIP THAT WHICH WE LOVE

Have you ever been infatuated with someone and felt so in love with that person that you just couldn't spend enough hours in the day with them? Like a drug, you sought after that person, calling them, sending them love messages, and your thoughts were occupied by that person all day long with little breaks of reality in between. God desires not only our obedience but our worship, as well. He wants us to desire Him, long for Him like a high school boy or girl with a crush.

Should we be obsessed with God? Should we be so taken with Him that we become fanatical zealots who cannot carry on regular lives, who wind up wandering the streets without jobs, abandoning everything else? Of course not. But God desires our worship, and we worship the things we love. One who has a great deal of money checks his stocks on a regular basis. A mother who loves her children spends a great deal of time with them, nurturing, caring for, and loving them. As Christians, we should be enamored with God and enjoy time spent with Him. Like a glass of ice water on a one hundred degree day, we must thirst and long for communion with the living God (Psalms 42:1).

If we love God, we are going to want to know all about Him. Like a lover longs to know his beloved, we should desire to understand the intimate details of God—all of Him. How do we come to know Him? We know God by studying, meditating upon, and contemplating Him often. Meditation means mulling God's Word over and over in your mind, allowing it to sink in and thinking about it after you have read it—like rewinding your favorite song. As you replay the message in your mind, you will not only infuse the information in your brain, but you will understand the information from every perspective and every angle, and your heart will begin to wrap around each truth. The next time you are studying the scripture, try taking only two or three verses, meditating upon them, and allowing them to sink in. God's Word is rich and should be savored deeply for the full flavor and the complete understanding of it. To know God we must invest time in the pursuit of Him.

God is jealous. He devoted the first two commandments to worshipping Him alone. Twenty percent of the commandments given to His people focus on the importance of devoting one's self to God more than anything else. Why do you think God put so much emphasis on this? One of the most damning elements of our society and lifestyles is the fact that we have so many distractions. Idolatry is the worship of, or devotion to, anything other than God. We commit idolatry when our priorities get rearranged and God takes a back seat rather than sitting upon the throne of our life where He belongs. Phone calls, e-mails, text messages, music, work, even our children, can distract us from our devotion to God. We have important priorities that require our attention. Marriage, parenting, and our careers are important, but God must be first in everything. He demands it. He deserves it. He is worthy of our devotion.

One of the first seminary classes I attended was a beginner theology class. In it, the professor mentioned he was aware that most students come to seminary with unanswered, nagging questions to which they longed for answers. I waited my turn and embarrassingly prepared my question.

> "I realize this may sound blasphemous to say, but if God is perfect, why isn't He humble? If Jesus was humble, even to the point of death, it just doesn't make sense to me why God requires so much devotion. He doesn't really need anything from us, so why does He demand we bow to Him and demand we praise Him?"

The professor hesitated, obviously heightening my nervousness for asking such a seemingly profane question, and began his response. "God desires our praise because He is worthy of it. He is God. He is almighty. The very nature of who God is demands our respect, our awe, and our devotion. It is not a violation of his character for God to desire being worshipped because He is God. In a nutshell—He deserves it." What an answer!

Since God is worthy of our devotion, we are responsible for being committed to Him. God gives us the freedom to act, to behave, and to think as individuals. He does not control our decisions or behavior. While God can allow consequences from our decisions, we are not merely puppets on strings. With this freedom, however, comes responsibility. We choose our friends, our spouses, our careers, our priorities, and to whom we are devoted. If my wife loved me only because she had signed a marriage certificate and only because I was the father of our children, would that be true love? Absolutely not. Which is better, for a wife to have to remind her husband that her birthday is next Tuesday, or for him to surprise her with a gift and arrange for a babysitter so they can have an evening together? How much more valuable for her husband to remember, to naturally be devoted to her without the need for being reminded? God wants our devotion to be second nature, to be a part of who we are.

One of the most intimate experiences I have ever had with God came at a time when I was very frustrated. I found myself at one of the many crossroads in my life, and I had been seeking direction from God for an extended period of time. I was beside myself with longing, desperate to hear from God before making an important decision. I prayed, studied the scripture, and did everything in my power to negotiate a response from God. I remember sitting in my car one night in the driveway, praying out loud, and I felt compelled to open my Bible. Of course, I do not normally open the scripture and point to a particular passage—like scriptural roulette—but this time I began to flip through scripture and something caught my attention in 1 Kings.

Elijah was upset and felt alone. God spoke to him and told him,

> "Go out and stand on the mountain in the presence of the Lord, for the Lord is about to pass by." Wind tore the mountains apart and shattered the rocks, but God was not in the wind. Then came an earthquake that shook the mountain, but God was not in the earthquake. Then came a sweeping fire, but God was not in the fire. But after all that came a *gentle whisper*, and Elijah covered his face with his cloak as God began to speak" (1 Kings 19).

I remember weeping, thinking myself so impertinent as to demand anything from God. Who am I to ask for a lightening bolt from the sky to come down with a note tied to it? God does not need our approval. He does not speak the way we want. He whispers gently in our ear, and it is our responsibility to listen. God is not a genie in a bottle or a vending machine where we put our quarters in and expect an answer, like our favorite candy bar, to drop in the slot. He is God! Mighty, perfect, holy, and infinite, yet willing to whisper in the ear of a little speck like me. Are we listening?

In our chaotic lifestyles, we find so little time to listen to God. If we really want to know Him, we must change our lifestyle. We must simplify our lives, slow down, and carve out time to spend with our creator. We have to spend less time talking and more time listening, studying scripture, and waiting upon the Lord. At every crossroad, with every major decision, in every difficult circumstance in our lives, God is working, leaning in, and calling us closer to Him. If we want to know Him, we have to give Him our full attention.

Have you ever talked to a young person and noticed the emphasis is always upon *them*? The conversation will often be ten percent of their concern about you and ninety percent focused on their lives—where they are going, what they are doing, their friends, their hair, their grades, their direction. We expect that because they are young. They are busy doing all they can to keep up with their own issues. Unfortunately, we are the same way when it comes to our relationship with God. We talk and talk in prayer but rarely listen. We forget that our relationship with God is not merely about receiving, but connecting, not only concentrating on our own needs but knowing and understanding who God really is. We are weak—frail with malnutrition from focusing on ourselves rather than focusing on God. A change is needed, and our lives must be altered if we are to attempt to understand God and know our maker.

God leaves room for us to choose to spend time with Him; He waits for us and has a divine appointment with us every day. If the president of the United States called to tell you he wanted to meet with you in your home today, what would you do? In my case, I would turn the house upside down trying to clean, rearrange furniture to hide stains, put on my best clothing, and try to be prepared. Would you blow off the appointment? Would you say, "Nah, thanks, anyway"?

God stretched out the heavens, drew the boundary lines for the oceans, and created everything we see in nature and all matter—the materials for what man has manufactured. With the words of His mouth, He spoke the world into existence. He is infinitely worthy of our devotion. If He is willing to stoop down and meet with us, how much more should we stop everything we are doing and concentrate on what He has to say?

He speaks through the scriptures. His Holy Spirit unites with our minds and calls to memory that which we have learned. He calms our hearts, takes away our guilt and shame, and replaces it with peace and deep, abiding joy. Why would we neglect so great a Father who loves us unconditionally? Distraction, chaos, all the good and important things in our lives need to be harnessed, simplified and prioritized, so we can efficiently get them done and still allow God the devotion He is due. Move toward efficiency, effectiveness, and organization. Say *no* to the things in your life that are not completely necessary. Don't eliminate them completely, but put limits on the leisurely activities in your life. Keep only what is most important and eliminate the fluff. Give God the time, devotion, and resources due Him first. The great reformer Martin Luther once said, "I have so much to do today, I shall spend the first three hours in prayer."

TO LOVE GOD IS TO KNOW GOD

God is infinite, immeasurable, and fathomless. Trying to wrap our minds around God is like drinking from a fire hydrant. Trying to describe God is like trying to explain the beauty of the Grand Canyon. Words and pictures all seem deficient and inadequate in describing a being who always was, always is, and always will be. The sharpest Bible scholar, the most eloquent writer, or the most talented artist has difficulty helping us truly understand who God really is. As Billy Graham put it, "Can you see God? Have you ever seen Him? I've never seen the wind! I've seen the effects of the wind, but I've never seen the wind." In the same way, we are only able to understand God from a distance. We cannot comprehend the whole scope of God. We can, however, concentrate on the essential attributes of God and attempt to put together a working model or, however limited, picture of God that will help us understand Him.

Most are familiar with the three inherent elements of God—His omnipotence, omniscience, and omnipresence. He has all the power, has all the knowledge, and is everywhere at the same time. With God's power, it is helpful to understand that though He created matter and the laws of nature, He is not limited to those laws. He created scientific laws to allow order, but He is not restricted by them. In other words, He transcends nature. He is *supernatural*. He is fully capable of suspending those laws as He sees fit, raising Jesus from the dead, stopping time twice, performing miraculous healings, feeding five thousand families with five fish and two loaves of bread, and other miracles (Joshua 10, 2 Kings 2, Matthew 14).

God has all wisdom—the beginning and the end of all knowledge. He knows everything there is to know—that which mankind has yet to discover. God's creative knowledge allowed Him to create plant life, animals, human beings, the constellations, and all the intricacies of every living as well as non-living entity. His ways are above our own (Isaiah 55).

God is everywhere at the same time and is capable of understanding every person since the beginning of time. He knows our thoughts, never sleeps, and is fully aware of every move we make, and nothing goes beyond His watchful eyes. God knows us and is familiar with all our ways. He formed us individually and knit us together while we were in the womb (Psalms 139:13).

God is infinitely merciful. His love has no bounds or limits, yet His love and mercy do not contradict His holiness, His sense of justice, and His wrath. God pours out His wrath on sin, and His justice has been served once and for all by the sacrifice of Jesus Christ on the cross. The perfect blood of Jesus was our atonement—our pardon for sin for all time. God is able to relate to

His children in love, even though we fail because Jesus's sacrifice paid the penalty that was due for sin (Romans 5:8). God's love is perfect, His ways are perfect, and He is absolutely holy. Yet God loves us unconditionally, as a mother her child, and if we have committed ourselves to Him through Jesus Christ, then we will never be parted from Him. We are forever engraved on the palms of His hands, and nothing can snatch us away from Him (Isaiah 49; John 10).

God considers us His children and offers us his unmerited grace as a result. Grace means He favors us. He is for us rather than against us. He does not stand in heaven like a bully on an ant hill with a magnifying glass, waiting to consume us with His wrath. When we make mistakes, God is grieved, but He does not act out in anger. He does not live to punish us for our mistakes. Rather, He is saddened when He is forced to allow the consequences of our sin to be experienced (Exodus 34). God is full of compassion for His hapless sheep that constantly go astray.

Finally, God is only approachable because of Christ's sacrifice. In the Old Testament, the Israelites who touched the mountain of God were struck dead! His holiness demands respect, awe, and reverence. If we were to actually see God, we would, like Isaiah, tremble with fear. Like Job, we would cry out, "My ears had heard of you but now my eyes have seen you. Therefore, I despise myself and repent in dust and ashes" (Job 42:5-6).

Without physically experiencing the magnitude, the beauty, and the breathtaking splendor of God, we cannot even conceive who He really is. Young persons often use the word "awesome" to describe a good movie, great song, or even a delicious meal. We have lost that sense of wonder and have no concept of what awesome truly is. The invisible, incredible God does not need man's consent or approval for anything, or even man's adoration, to prove Himself. He does not need scientific proof to validate the reality of His existence. God simply is the great *I Am*. The sooner we acknowledge it and concede to His authority in our lives, the healthier we will be—emotionally and spiritually.

I encourage you to engage in a study of the names of God given by the Hebrews in the Old Testament. They give much insight and comfort and remind us of all that God is and all He does. When we truly understand the God we serve, we experience the complete peace that accompanies faith in our creator. Knowing God fully results in a life filled with confidence in His sovereignty, regardless of the circumstances we face from one day to the next.

BECOMING A CROSS-BEARER

Many people claim to be believers in God. Of those who profess to have faith, only a select few acknowledge faith through Jesus Christ. For many who claim to be "spiritual," even stating the words "Jesus" and "Christ" back to back in a sentence, bring feelings of anxiety or even shame. Among evangelical believers in Christ, there are even fewer who are what could be considered to be true disciples of Christ. A disciple is one who intensely follows Jesus and feels compelled to adhere to the Holy Scriptures. In short, a disciple is one who is willing to deny herself, take up the cross, and follow Jesus. Denying what she wants, a disciple says, "Not my will but yours be done" (Luke 22:42).

Disciples may have success as the world sees it such as fame, thriving careers, or accomplishments, but they do not measure success in that manner. A disciple's goal is to please God, and they work toward that end diligently. Life decisions, like career and goals, all revolve around God's desires rather than their own. A disciple truly understands the scripture in Psalms that reads, "Delight yourself in the Lord and He will give you the desires of your heart" (Psalms 37:4). A disciple's desires are in tune with God's, and since their lives are surrendered totally to Him, their goals coincide beautifully with Christ's path for their lives.

What are your dreams? Do you desire material wealth, worldly success, fame, glory, or the American Dream? God may have all those things planned for you. That might be exactly His will for your life—or it may not. Are you willing to sacrifice everything, all that you hold dear, for the sake of Christ? If you truly want to be His disciple, one for whom the world holds no sway, you must have a loose grip on the things you consider important on this earth. If you truly desire to go deeper, to walk more closely with God, you must be willing to allow God to plow up the hard ground in your heart, find those places you are grudgingly grasping, and let them go.

Does that mean God desires you to be an ascetic martyr who becomes so fanatical in your faith that you become useless for the kingdom of God, unable to relate to a fallen world? In America, I would guess that few in the faith would find themselves in danger of falling into that category. There are, however, people who favor legalism and are bound by the notion that they must earn the favor of God. Those who grind it out every day, attempting to buy God's clemency for their sins, have no notion of the grace of God (Ephesians 2). What a miserable existence, to feel as though you must constantly work, day by day, to make it to heaven. With all the mistakes we make, how burdensome would it be to constantly have to counter them with good deeds? Like a rat in an exercise wheel, we would be constantly running, straining to cancel out sins, all the while committing new ones every day.

God desires holiness, however, and while we are never going to achieve complete purity this side of heaven, we are commissioned by God to work toward it nonetheless. Jesus said, "Anyone who desires to come after me must deny himself, take up his cross, and follow me" (Luke 9:23). We often glorify the cross itself, wearing it as jewelry around our necks and symbolizing it as though it were something inherently holy. Would we wear jewelry with a guillotine or an electric chair on it? The cross is a symbol of the cruel, horrible, torturous death our savior endured to wipe away our sin. It was gruesome, inhumane, vile, and a cursed way to die. Just as those who commit horrible crimes live forever in disgrace, the cross was meant to represent something ugly, the shameful manner in which God had to deal with sin. When Jesus commanded His disciples to take up their cross, He meant to identify with His suffering, to endure the difficulties of the Christian walk as Jesus did—obedient unto death. Discipleship means death to self, death to our desires, and willingness to bear the difficult burdens of this Christian life.

At the same time, discipleship is a wonderful means of becoming a true believer, of learning how to walk as Jesus did. It was Jesus' method of reaching the world for Christ. As some in the faith have said, there was no plan B. Jesus ministered to thousands, but He had a select few with whom He was intimately related. He poured His life into the twelve. While one defected, the other eleven were not only well acquainted with

Him, but they knew His ways and witnessed how He daily carried out His faith.

Scripture is all-important, but learning it and attaining knowledge of it is entirely different than living it in real life. Just as medical interns have a doctor watching them practice, correcting them, and showing them how to hone their skills, we as Christians need someone to help us understand how to walk faithfully and how to practice real-life Christianity. I will never forget the director of Campus Outreach, an interdenominational ministry at my college, pouring his life into me. The impact he had on my life is immeasurable—all the freezing mornings he left his warm bed and trudged over to my dorm room only to have to wake me up to have a quiet time. What a sacrifice that was! And after all the hard work of pouring his life into me—only to see me fall away from the faith for a time—it must have been frustrating for him. But his ministry, his kindness, and most importantly, the principles of scripture I saw him exhibit in everyday life have never lost their impact on me.

There is no better way to reach others for Christ, to help them along in their walk with Christ, than discipleship. Do you have a mentor? Are you spending time with someone older or younger than you in the faith? If not, you are not only missing out on fulfilling your potential as a believer and the accountability that could keep you on fire for God, but you are also denying yourself the opportunity to fulfill the great commission, helping win the world for Christ.

THOMAS C. BATES, M.S.

Loving God involves being singly devoted to Him, and loving others means we must connect in a genuine way with real people. What better way to practice the ultimate command by connecting with those who have more experience and allowing them to share that wisdom through discipleship? Finally, pouring our lives into others is the deepest way to express love, to connect in a heartfelt way with another. Make your life count by passing on what you have learned, and allowing those older than you in the faith to do the same for you.

THE RED PHONE

Have you ever seen a spy movie where the agency has a red phone in which they are able to contact the president at any moment? Can you imagine the ability to contact the leader of the free world at a moment's notice whenever a crisis in your life arose? God is available, willing to help at a second's notice. He has an answer for every question, every situation, and He does not desire for us to suffer in silence.

We are in a position of great importance in the eyes of God. He longs for us to seek Him, to recognize His ability to calm the storms of life, and to give us aid when we need it most. Though every situation in our life is under His control, He waits patiently for us to admit our need for Him. He is already engaged, already helping, and already directing all our circumstances. But there is something to be said about our willingness to invite Him in, to acknowledge His sovereignty, and most importantly, confess our powerlessness to overcome without God's intervention.

So how should we pray? Jesus gave us a perfect example in Matthew 6. We should not seek to pray publicly to be acknowledged by others but rather to pray privately to God. When we do so, God will reward the prayer that is offered by faith to an unseen God. We do not need to go on and on, repeating ourselves and chattering meaninglessly. We should have something to say, believing God is listening and honoring Him with our faith. We must believe the fact that not only is God listening, but He will answer according to His will. Faith is a very important part of our prayer, and we cannot please God without it (Hebrews 11:6). In addition, we must recognize that God knows our thoughts and our desires before we ask. We ought to revere God's name, contemplating His holiness and the power of His name from the beginning of our prayer. We ought to express our gratitude for what He has done—giving us His attention for who He is. We ought to worship Him and magnify or extol His virtues and His holy attributes. We should acknowledge our desire to align ourselves with God's purposes. We should seek during prayer to find our part in His plan while expressing our desire to move in His direction rather than our own.

If you read Jesus's description of prayer in Matthew 6, He never mentions praying for a nice home, a big car, or a vacation. The only request of God is daily bread—daily provisions. Neither provision for tomorrow nor anything else material is mentioned—only enough for today. Jesus mentions our need to ask for forgiveness for our sin, but He also mentions we should forgive those who have sinned against us. Jesus takes time to explain the fact that if we do not forgive others who have sinned against us, God will not forgive our own sin. He also mentions prayer for protection from temptation and deliverance from Satan.

Simple, eloquent, comprehensive—this is the manner in which we should pray. There are other places in scripture that describe prayer, and I do not believe God would have us limit ourselves to praying exactly as Jesus did. This is a pattern in which we ought to pray—not an exclusive catechism from which we never deviate. First Thessalonians 5 says that we should give thanks in all circumstances, never neglecting the attitude of thankfulness—no matter what circumstances we are facing. I have often drawn from one example, among others, that uses the acronym "P-R-A-Y."

P—Praise God at the beginning of each prayer.

R—Repent, ask the Holy Spirit to reveal any unconfessed sin and take time to ask forgiveness and turn away from it.

A—Ask for that which you need according to God's will.

Y—Yield yourself to Him, to His purposes in your life.

Assume a posture of humility before the almighty God, acknowledge His wisdom to direct you, and acknowledge your desire to keep in step with His Spirit—His plan.

Jesus told us that if we ask anything in His name, according to His will, He would give it to us. This, of course, implies that we are asking with the right motives, in keeping with His plans and directives. The closer we draw near Him, the more accurate our desires, and the nearer our wishes will match His.

Just as a young adult slowly begins to understand and appreciate his parents' discipline in his life—the reasons for the curfews and the restrictions and the decisions that, at the time, seemed cruel—our understanding and appreciation of God's answers make sense when we become more mature in our faith.

Why, though, with so great a Savior, do we neglect our opportunity to call upon Him? Available at any moment, we have His ear, and yet we forget. It is as though our default mode is to operate in our own strength—to handle things on our own. We have His presence and the ability to call upon Him, and we rob ourselves of the opportunity to have God show up in the middle of our trials, in our relationship issues, and in the day-to-day activities of our lives. God is not aloof, as some believe. He is involved in the minute-by-minute issues we face. He wants us to pray often, to interact with Him continually (1 Thessalonians 5:17).

Another element of prayer I have learned is that God honors our intensity. The more we care about an issue and the more fervently we pray for something, God responds. God says, "You will seek me and find me when you seek me with all your heart" (Jeremiah 29:13). There are times when God responded swiftly, sometimes even immediately, in my life. Those have always been the times when I have been in a very urgent situation. During those intense moments of prayer when I cry out to Him in utter desperation, I have seen Him respond and have felt His Spirit flow through me like a welcome breeze on a miserably hot day. God honors us when we throw ourselves at His mercy, acknowledging our need for His immediate attention. While we always have His attention, He resonates with and responds more quickly to our deepest, most sincere, and desperate cries.

God is not sitting silently somewhere far away. He does not want us to walk through life alone, vainly stumbling through it in our own strength. Are you interacting with Him repeatedly throughout the day, or does your interaction with God only take place in your home? If that is the case, you are missing out on God's presence in your daily life. If you are leaving Him out of certain areas of your life, work, or social activities, not only do you risk vulnerability to the enemy's schemes, but you forfeit the chance to do great exploits for God. Lord forbid we should arrive at the end of our lives and suffer the regret of missed opportunity, a life filled with busy-*ness*, or a life focused on the earthly and the immediate, rather than the eternal.

NIAGARA FALLS AT YOUR FINGERTIPS

Imagine a woman, Linda, who gets a notice from the post office that a lost letter has been recovered. Somehow, it had been caught in a postal sorting machine, hidden for many years until it was finally discovered by a maintenance worker performing a thorough cleaning. Linda has been a widow for eight long years, struggling for income, having re-entered the workforce upon the death of her husband and being forced to raise her two children alone. Year after year she has wrestled with staying barely above the poverty level. Over and over, she has been evicted from her apartment, paying reconnection fees for utilities, driving a clunky vehicle on the verge of collapse, and living in an unsafe neighborhood.

Linda drives to the post office, expecting to see another bill she will be unable to pay, wondering if this will be the straw that breaks the camel's back, the final push over the edge into homelessness, despair and ruin. She opens the letter hesitantly, with all the gloom and despondency of a woman who has lived through countless calamities. To her surprise, the letter is from an attorney's office. She reads on, dumbfounded, and learns that a late uncle, whom she had never met, has left his entire estate to her! Millions of dollars, property, stocks—all of it—had been left in her name. There was no one else available—no other surviving heir. Everything belongs to her. No more struggles, no more fighting to survive from week to week. Her daughters can attend the finest schools. She will have a home and will be able to work only if she wants to do so. She could go to college and study art, something she has always wanted to do, and give to the church. "Oh, if I had only received this letter when it was sent, how much suffering I could have avoided!" she laments.

Did you know many of you are just like Linda? You have countless resources and ultimate power right at your fingertips. God owns the cattle on a thousand hills; everything is His. Everything we require is at His disposal. We must recognize the fact that God is infinitely capable of providing, healing, and restoring, regardless of our needs. Immeasurable wealth, capable of healing, delivering, overturning, reclaiming—God is proficient in every way. He can do it! Is there something in your life you feel incapable of overcoming? Are you struggling with a spouse, a child, or other loved one who refuses to change? Are you in a dead-end job with no hope in sight, or have you just watched your dreams go up in smoke? Are you or someone you love in need of physical healing? God can overcome any problem in your life or give you the strength to carry on in spite of what seems impossible.

There is a way through any predicament, with God's strength. God's Word says that when you struggle, He will not allow you to be tempted more than you can bear but will provide a way out from under it (1 Corinthians 10:13). That does not mean your situation will not be difficult or that you will not feel like giving up at times. God knows exactly what you need precisely when you need it. However, God's ways are higher than ours, and He allows circumstances to happen, which, at the time, may seem unfair or perhaps even cruel.

This is the stumbling block for so many unbelievers. They cannot get past the suffering God allows in the lives of His children. The established responses from those in the Christian faith do not satisfy these unbelievers. I have heard it said many times that sin is the source of all evil and is the reason for all of the problems in the world. If man had not sinned, we would not have to endure the terrible things in the world like sickness, crimes, disease, and death.

It is true that sin is the source of all evil, and every heartache we endure, every terrible thing that happens in the world, can be traced back to Adam and Eve and their exit from the garden. "So you are telling me my seven-year-old daughter died of cancer because of sin in the world? What did she do to deserve that? What kind of God would allow such abominations as starvation, physical and sexual abuse, and genocide?" No, we do not have answers as to why God allows such horrors to exist, and, yes, God does allow them. If He is truly in control, then He must be in control of everything—the good and the bad.

Our answers do not satisfy these questioners because we are not sovereign. We do not know everything—

only God does. There are times when we do not have a response to what is happening to us. And God is under no obligation to explain Himself to man. He is God. There is a plan, and God is in charge of it. We can speculate. We can try to make it add up, but sometimes it just doesn't.

While we may not have all the answers for the terrible things that happen to us, there are some things we *can* know for certain from the Word of God. In everything God does, He desires to draw us nearer to Him. Can you look back on your life and think about the times when you have been the closest to God? Those times when we are nearest to God are usually the phases in our lives when we struggle and when we hurt the most. When everything is rosy, we have no need for God, and our spiritual lives dwindle. So we can be sure that difficulties have one purpose—drawing, often driving, us to our knees.

While that may seem like involuntary servitude, it is a lesson that results in a resolute dependence upon and inseparable bond with God. Our faith grows, our grip on the temporal things of life loosens, and we learn to see the world around us as God does. We focus on things above, rather than the things of the earth. Our priorities change, and our strivings cease. We learn to be still and to enjoy life around us. In our weakness, God is able to shine.

When our pride is broken, our self-sufficiency declines, and God is free to release His creative power— His divine energy in our lives. We go, as Paul says, from faith to faith. I visualize that concept as going from one spiritual plateau to another, hopefully climbing, but sometimes declining, in our faith. How quickly, when adversity comes, do we forget the previous trials God has brought us through!

Adversity in our lives not only draws us nearer to God and strengthens our faith muscles but also makes us useful for the kingdom of God. A.W. Tozer said, "I doubt God can use anyone greatly until He has hurt them deeply." Think of a non-believer going through hard times, possibly engineered by God to help that person realize his need for a savior, encountering a Christian on his journey. Imagine a chipper Christian talking about how God is "so good to me" and how everything is perfect in his Christian world. All is right in the world, and this bubbly person just makes the non-believer sick to his stomach. *How could he possibly understand me? How could he understand what it is like to be in my shoes?* the non-believer thinks. *I don't believe he is real. I think he's living in a fantasy world.*

But what if, for example, God allows a non-believer who has recently lost a child to encounter a Christian who, sadly, has walked through the same dread, disillusionment, pain, or sorrow? Do you not think a non-believer would listen or be more apt to receive the Christian's testimony about how God brought him through such a horrible time in his life? One of the biggest reasons God allows pain and suffering is not only to teach us, draw us closer, and increase our faith, but He also allows us to be seasoned through grief to counsel and minister to others. No one is better equipped to minister to another than one who drank from the same bitter cup.

Above all, we need to remember that God desires to do great things in all of our lives. He has a plan, and we, are an integral part of it. Will you squander your opportunity for greatness by allowing past hurts, failures, and discouragements to suck you into the quicksand of despair? God wants to pluck you out of the mire and set your feet on solid ground. God wants you to be "seated with Christ in the heavenly realms" (Ephesians 1:20). Just as a pilot climbs above the storm and looks down upon it, when we set our mind on things above and focus on Christ, we can live above our circumstances, not only enduring, but thriving in the midst of adversity.

Regardless of the difficulties we face, God wants to connect with us. It is in linking ourselves to God where we not only find peace but the path and purpose, the direction we need to move forward. Connect with God, draw from His vast resources and drink deeply, you will find whatever you seek.

LOVING YOURSELF

One of the last portions of the ultimate command often goes unnoticed. You are called to love your neighbor as yourself (Matthew 22:39). That can seem contradictory to most individuals because it seems selfish to love oneself. There are many in the Christian faith who seem to take a particularly ascetic view of themselves. They equate spirituality with self-denial so much so as to think of themselves as mere worms, worthy of only pain, suffering, and woe. Yes, Christ does advocate for "denying oneself and taking up the cross" (Luke 9:23). God *does* promote the prayer in which one beats his breast and says, "Have mercy on me," over one who condescendingly prays like the Pharisee, "God, I thank you that I am not like other men—robbers, evildoers, adulterers—or even like this tax collector" (Luke 18:11). But God does not advocate for denying oneself absolutely. We are called by Paul in scripture to be soberminded, to not think "more highly of ourselves than we should" (Romans 12:3). Yet here it is, in scripture, in the ultimate command: we are called to love others "as ourselves." It is not a suggestion but a command.

Does that mean we are to become narcissistic, looking down upon the world as unworthy and worshipping ourselves above all others? No. But it does not mean we are worms, unworthy of love, beyond repair, beyond hope, or worthless. There is a healthy balance between pride and self-love and thinking of oneself as insignificant. We are not pledges in the fraternity of humankind, bound as Christians to a life of servitude without value.

No, we do not deserve the grace bestowed upon us as believers or the mercy applied by the blood of Christ. We deserve punishment for our sins and spiritual death and the flames of hell for all the mistakes we have made. But more often than not, many of us forget who we are and what has been done for us. We forget and, therefore, trample upon the blood that was shed for us as believers in Christ. Do you struggle like me, with forgiving yourself? Do you believe in scripture, in the atoning sacrifice of Christ? Every time you allow Satan to skew your thinking, to make you believe you are a worm, you trample on the blood of Christ. You are nullifying Christ's death for you when you forget your appointed station and when you forget that Christ has declared you righteous in God's eyes.

God sees you through glasses that are stained with the blood of Christ. Do you remember when as a child you would pull the plastic bag out of the cereal box to get to the toy inside? I remember one toy that I loved as a child; it was a set of secret spy decoder glasses. There would be hidden messages with a special color ink on the back of the cereal box that could not be detected with the naked eye. But with your secret spy decoder glasses, you could read the secret message that no one else could see.

We need to realize that God has special vision. Like that message no one else could read, He sees you in a way no one else can. He sees your potential. He sees what will be. He sees you the way you would be without sin. He sees you the way a mother of a convicted felon often sees her son. While the whole world is angry with the serial-killer, child molester, liar, thief, or other manner of law-breaker, his mother sees him as the child she raised—unspoiled by the world before he made all the wrong choices—as her precious son.

We look upon that convicted felon as a menace. Many of us want to see him punished so the victims can be vindicated—and rightly so. But we are so much like that law-breaker. Measured against the perfection and holiness of God, how do we compare? Have you ever taken office supplies from work, omitted income on your taxes, or held back the facts when telling your side of the story? Have you ever wished someone could be demoted in life, "taken down a notch," refused to forgive someone who hurt you or restore a relationship when it was in your power to do so? Have you looked down upon a homeless person, one who struggles with continual addiction with a critical heart, perceiving they are just weak? Maybe you have felt the pang of jealousy and covetousness riding down the road and seeing that stately home, asking yourself, "Why do they get to live like that, when will I ever get to have nice things?" There is very little difference between us and the convicted felon in the eyes of God. We all have fallen short of God's best for us, and are guilty of covet-ousness, judging others, and unforgiveness among others. God does not place a higher penalty upon one sin over another.

Yes, we have failed and have faltered, and we often do so over and over again. We are helpless at times and some of us have been, and even *are* today, addicted and racked with enormous guilt over continued bouts with sin in our lives. Day after day, we grapple with the old nature inside us. We often cry out, like Paul, "Oh wretched man [or woman] I am! Who will rescue me from this body of death?" (Romans 7:24).

Addiction, weaknesses, and habitual and recurring sins that plague us often cause us to doubt our salvation, calling into question whether or not faith is real and whether or not God is real. This battle with which we struggle pulls us into a tailspin that seems almost impossible to restore. But we have to find, hold onto, digest, and make as a permanent part of our thinking the powerful, irrefutable truths of scripture. I ask again—do you believe the Holy Scriptures? The Bible says, "God is faithful and just to forgive us" (1 John 1:9). He is faithful to do it. He will not fail to forgive again and again. He has the right to do so, for it does not conflict with His sense of justice, holiness, and perfection because of Christ's death on the cross. The blood of Christ cleanses us.

Am I saying that habitual sin is acceptable—that Christians can be addicted, have continual sin with which they struggle, and still be considered genuine Christians? I am not certain, but I believe it is pos-

THOMAS C. BATES, M.S.

sible. Just as an alcoholic often remains in recovery for the rest of their lives, remembering their weakness and understanding the dangers of addiction, people are not always delivered completely from temptation or tendencies toward particular sinful behaviors.

In some cases, devout believers have come to the conclusion that these sinful behaviors are a result of not having been a Christian in the first place. These people believe their conversion wasn't real, and they did not have a genuine life-altering faith experience or ever actually surrendered control of their lives to Christ. Regardless, true Christians will never be comfortable with sin in their lives. If they are engaged in a habit that is truly sinful, a true believer will never genuinely overcome the guilt that accompanies this behavior.

Many in the faith will depart from me on this point and say that a true believer cannot be addicted to anything or have continual sin and been a real convert in the first place. I could argue my point further, but this debate will go on and on until Christ comes back. I will conclude the point by saying that Paul was a believer when he wrote Romans 7, and he would not, under the inspiration of Scripture, have written that he engaged in the very sin he hated or committed the very things he did not want to do if we as believers were not subject to continual struggles with specific, persistent sin in our lives.

How are we to reconcile all this? What are we to do about it? How can we find the balance between thinking too lowly of ourselves and thinking too loftily about ourselves? We must use the healthy guilt that drives us to do better and dispense with unhealthy guilt that sends us shooting downward into a cycle of shame. We need to remember God's promises. We need to sink our teeth into, process, and become one with the realities of Scripture, allowing them to become such a part of us that they remind us who we are when the world, the devil, and our own brain tries to tell us otherwise.

Like the pardoned criminal who values what has been done for him, we should spend the rest of our lives being grateful for the multitude of *slates* God has cleaned. If you have been locked in the dungeon of shame or if you have been racked by guilt, even as you read these words, stop! Accept the grace that is yours. You are right if you say you don't deserve it—absolutely right. But it is yours, my friend. You need only accept it. Don't say that God could never forgive you. That is a lie from the pit of hell, as though Satan himself said it.

We still haven't completely answered the question of how we live on a daily basis with guilt, taking from it the good, allowing it to spur us on to becoming better, and preventing ourselves from allowing our shame to get us off track. We have discussed understanding God's forgiveness and how He views us—but what about from a human perspective? How do we truly become a person who loves himself in a healthy, balanced, non-narcissistic way? The foundation lies in understanding our value and our importance in the eyes of God, and I think this is a worthy pursuit, a project, and a Bible study that should last a lifetime. Nevertheless, there are some practical methods that can be beneficial to us, as well.

THOMAS C. BATES, M.S.

In the book *Changes that Heal*, Henry Cloud has an excellent example that is invaluable in achieving a healthy view of ourselves (Cloud 1992).[3] He believes every person has two individual parts: an ideal self and a real self. Take Jim, for example. The perfect Jim never yells at the kids and loves and cares for his wife perfectly. The ideal Jim is always on time, never forgets important details, never loses anything, always pleases God, and never struggles with sin. At the end of the day, perfect Jim has everything accomplished. The ideal Jim pleases everyone, never feels inadequate, and never experiences failure in any way.

Then there is the real Jim—the one who drops the ball and who constantly blows it on a daily basis. The real Jim has to apologize to his wife and children for getting angry, and to his boss for making mistakes at work. At the end of every day, the real Jim always leaves something undone and always experiences some form of failure. For Jim, the key to having a healthy sense of self-worth is by focusing on the ideal part of himself, working toward the person he wants to be.

The same is true for us. If you see something that doesn't measure up to the ideal, then concentrate on changing that aspect of your life. But in your pursuit of the ideal self, remember that you are human. You must be able to look at yourself in the mirror and cut yourself some slack. You must make peace with this process, make peace with your real self, and be able to give yourself grace, accepting the fact that you are a sinner—a "work in progress." Don't waste energy beating yourself up. Instead, direct that energy toward changing. If you are working toward change, tell yourself the truth. You are moving in a positive direction and you are getting better. Believe in God's sovereignty and His powerful Holy Spirit inside you and remember this wonderful verse, "For I am confident of this, that He who began a good work in you will perfect it until the day of Christ" (Philippians 1:6).

God is at work in us. He is changing us day-by-day, and He is ultimately responsible for our becoming more like Himself. Trust Him to do it. And remember the fact that God sees us as the perfected individuals we are to be, looking past our failures and applying the blood of Christ to our lives. We have been declared righteous, not by anything we have done or by any merit on our part but because of His great love for us. It is very easy to give ascent to this truth and to understand it, but to make it a part of who we are is a different story. We have to constantly remind ourselves of the grace of God—of His mercy and forgiveness. We must be balanced in our thinking. We need not deny the inner voice of God telling us we are wrong, and at the same time we must not wallow in a pond of guilt. We cannot allow negative thinking, past failures, and regret to prevent us from moving forward, away from the great things God wants us to achieve.

Finally, we must always remember God wants to, can, and *will* forgive us. Like the father of the prodigal looking down the road every day for his son, God longs to welcome you back into His arms (Luke 15). No matter how many times, no matter what others think of you, and no matter what you think of yourself, He is faithful and just. He will carry out your forgiveness, and He can because of the blood He allowed His son to spill on your behalf. But you must accept it. Release the devil's stranglehold on you, keeping you down by denying yourself the forgiveness you don't deserve. Accept it right now. Today—this very instant.

CAPTURING SURRENDERED GROUND

This chapter brings us to the most important aspect concept of loving ourselves, the practical means by which you will be able to effect change in your life. If you want to take charge of your life, remove the shackles of guilt, shame, worry or fear you need a thought plan. What in the world is a "thought plan," anyway? A thought plan is a method for transforming your thinking, a metamorphosis from negativity, fear, worry, unhealthy guilt to a positive, hope-filled life. As a woman or man thinks, so is (s)he. Pick three times per day that you will remind yourself to check your thinking. Try mealtimes or three situations in which you regularly find yourself doing a similar activity. Use those times to check your thinking, looking back to check your progress, reminding yourself to be on your guard in the coming hours. Put notes in prominent places to remind yourself to check your thoughts.

Ask yourself these questions, "Am I thinking correctly? Am I telling myself the truth? Am I working toward correcting this particular issue with which I am dealing?" If you aren't, use this time to correct yourself. Don't waste emotional energy focusing on the negative or beating yourself up, just move toward the positive, one step at a time. Move toward fixing what is wrong. Give yourself credit when you succeed even in the smallest way, and don't waste time punishing yourself. Keep telling yourself the truth—"I am going to overcome this. Little by little, I am going to succeed, I am going to accomplish it—no matter how long it takes."

Josh has been struggling with guilt. Since his fiancé left him he wonders if he will ever find love again. He blames himself for the breakup and struggles with self-worth, is unsure about his career, and feels like he has no future. In utter desperation, he decides to see a counselor, who recommends a daily thought plan.

At first, Josh has trouble remembering to check his thinking three times a day. After a week, he finally remembers the counselor asked him to put notes in prominent places. He buys some sticky notes, writes the message *How is your thinking?* in bold letters and puts them on his mirror in the bathroom, on his fridge, on his desk at work and on the dash of his car. In addition, he writes Philippians 4:8 on an index card to memorize.

During breakfast, he reminds himself that he is not a loser, but a child of God for whom Christ died, and remembers God has a plan for him. During the day, when he feels those longings for his fiancé and the pain, he remembers that he has learned from this failure, he will be a better man for it. He remembers where he went wrong, and says to himself, "I will learn how to treat a girl right, and something good will come of this." After lunch, when the loneliness creeps in, he cautions himself against feelings of self-pity. He says to himself, "Josh, you are not alone, God is with you and enough to meet your needs." In the evening, when he goes home alone and begins to feel down about the size of his apartment and his prospects for the future, he remembers to look online at a college in which he is interested.

Over time, Josh begins to build healthier habits in his thinking. He still occasionally struggles with loneliness, beating himself up about the break-up, but these times become less frequent. He begins to get out more, connects with healthy friends, actually begins to identify some life-long goals and takes steps in moving towards them.

A thought plan can be a most powerful ally in the war against negative thinking. Changing your thought patterns can help you overcome fear, anxiety, panic, compulsive behavior, and depressive thinking. Healthy thinking can give you the power to tip the scales from self-loathing, feeling miserable, and lacking self-control to a confident, purposeful, hopeful and inspired life.

When I think of emotional healing, deliverance from destructive thought, or behavior patterns, I am reminded of Gandalf's words to the king of Rohan in the *The Lord of the Rings: The Two Towers* (Tolkien 1993).[4] After dispelling Saruman's hold on his mind, Gandalf said, "Breathe the free air." Do you want to breathe the free air? Do you want freedom from addiction, recurrent sin, poor self-worth, lack of self-control, and to have deliverance from negative thinking? You must take advantage of this all-important tool.

THOMAS C. BATES, M.S.

Do you want to breathe freely again? Memorize this valuable message from Philippians, sometimes referred to as the "Philippians 4:8 filter." Memorize this verse— "Finally, brothers, whatever is true, whatever is noble, whatever is right, whatever is pure, whatever is lovely, whatever is admirable—if anything is excellent or praiseworthy—think about such things."

You cannot control the thoughts that pop into your head, but you can control what you allow to rattle around in there. Anger, bitterness, jealousy, contempt, un-forgiveness, fear, discouragement, anxiety, depressive, negative thoughts about yourself or someone else, and those things that you know are not healthy, filter them out. The thoughts that you know are pure, admirable, noble, true, lovely—those that belong—allow them to pass through the filter.

The Bible says we are to take every thought captive to the obedience of Christ. Like a mother who takes hold of her child as he strains toward the street for his ball, you must take hold of those thoughts and not let them go. We are called to grab those unhealthy thoughts rattling around in our head and keep them from causing pain. The mind is the enemy's battleground and the place where he often causes the most damage. If we grasp this concept, put it into practice, and begin to tell ourselves the truth, we can overcome the majority of our issues.

Randy Carlson, founder of *Parent Talk on Call*, once said, "You behave your way into situations, and you must behave your way out of them. If you have negative behavior patterns, thinking isn't enough. Like this concept I have tried to describe, if you want to overcome and have the power to see change in your lives, you must not just think about it but *do something* about it. Little by little, step by step, one day at a time, move toward that which you want to accomplish, and eventually you will get better." Since we are creatures of habit, we must realize it will take time to develop healthier thinking patterns. It is very important to continue working, to keep focusing on building these good habits over time.

How we think, our attitude, is critical in the level of happiness, contentment, and even sanity we experience. A cheerful heart really is good medicine, and a crushed spirit truly does dry up the bones (Proverbs 17:22). Feelings of hopelessness and despairing thoughts compound each other. When you allow yourself to lose hope and when you spiral downward in your thinking, it opens the door to the enemy's attacks. Your body often responds, as well, which sometimes raises your blood pressure, causing stomach and digestive problems and stress on your heart, too. If we are to fulfill the ultimate command, we must love not only God and others, but love and take care of ourselves.

The two areas over your life over which you control your own life are these: your thoughts and your attitude. God gives us free will, and you have a choice to make. Will you choose happiness, hope, and faith to get you through this life? Or will you drown in your own sorrow, becoming a bitter hopeless soul squandering your life, and sucking the life from those around you until the end. Read and soak in the wonderful quote from Chuck Swindoll called *Attitude*.

THOMAS C. BATES, M.S.

The longer I live, the more I realize the impact of attitude on life. Attitude, to me, is more important than facts. It is more important than the past, the education, the money, than circumstances, than failure, than successes, than what other people think or say or do. It is more important than appearance, giftedness or skill. It will make or break a company... a church... a home. The remarkable thing is we have a choice everyday regarding the attitude we will embrace for that day. We cannot change our past... we cannot change the fact that people will act in a certain way. We cannot change the inevitable. The only thing we can do is play on the one string we have, and that is our attitude. I am convinced that life is 10% what happens to me and 90% of how I react to it. And so it is with you... we are in charge of our Attitudes" (Swindoll 2011).[5]

One last example I will share is this: we are all creatures of habit. I have a history, one that was, unfortunately, passed down to me by my mother's side of the family of being scatter-brained and forgetting important details, events, and items like wallets, keys, and cell phones. I know it is hereditary because my mother speaks of my grandfather often losing his wallet while plowing a field, and my mother and her siblings had to walk the fields and look for it. My mother often forgets events and loses things, as well.

Have you ever had a character trait that became a pet peeve of yours, but you seemed powerless to overcome? My wife and children will testify to the fact that when I misplace something, when something gets lost, I lose my cool; I will not rest until it is found. I hate losing things. I made up my mind years ago that I would do something about it. I decided I would do my best to put my keys and wallet in the same place every day, so as not to lose them. So I embarked on a new journey to establish a habit of doing that, every day placing my keys and wallet in the top drawer of my dresser. Time and time again, I would forget, but I just kept trying, doing my best to avoid beating myself up when I forgot but continuing to focus on building that habit. Now, I don't want to jinx myself here, but guess what? In the last ten years, I can say that I have rarely, almost *never* lost my wallet—maybe two or three times have I lost my keys, wallet, or cell phone. But I have achieved some success, and I honestly feel good about it.

Why have I said all this? Because for the thinking plan to work, anything you want to change, needs to be built into a habit, little by little and day after day. Just keep focusing on the goal, striving toward it, and moving in a healthy direction. Eventually, over time, you will look back and see that there are more days you succeed than you fail, and let that launch you into newfound confidence and courage to improve other areas of your life. Remember to make peace with your real self, using the ideal self to help you improve those areas with which you are not happy. God has commanded us to love yourself, and when you beat yourself up, spiral downward, or forget your position in Christ, you are disobeying God!

FLEXING OUR SPIRITUAL MUSCLES

How many of you have started New Year's resolutions only to have them crumble by mid-February? I am no stranger to that concept. I start with the best intentions, only to allow outside circumstances, life, to interrupt my goals, squelch my enthusiasm, watching my self-discipline fall like a house of cards. How can I be healthy? If my body is a temple, then I would liken it to the leaning (and I might add balding and bulging) tower of Pizza Hut! But there are other areas of my life that lack discipline, too.

God has called us to be disciplined. While there are exceptions, I would venture to guess many, if not most, of the followers of Christ have forgotten the lost art of fasting. Fasting was a regular routine of Jews in Old Testament times and is still followed by many orthodox Jews today. Americans, however, rarely deny themselves food as a means by which one can become more focused on God. While I do not believe in asceticism, many disciplines, like fasting, are very helpful and may be excellent ways to establish discipline in our lives.

Biblical fasting usually meant avoiding food from sunup to sundown and, as described by Jesus, was meant to be kept hidden from others—not to be displayed outwardly. Jesus explained that people who fasted were to wear typical clothing, wash themselves, and treat their appearance no different than if they weren't fasting. The point of fasting is to deny oneself food and to establish discipline over one's hunger as a sacrifice to God. Rather than focus on filling one's belly, fasting challenges us to focus on God, instead. Are you looking for a spiritual breakthrough? Do you want deliverance from some sin? Are you at a crossroad in your life and need specific direction from God? I highly recommend fasting as a means to commune with God. Some of the most powerful spiritual moments in my life, including the writing of this book, were done while focusing on God more than food. And if you knew how much I love food, you would know that, for me, fasting is a spiritual discipline which requires extra special effort.

In addition to fasting, one of the deepest disciplines I believe we ignore is that of deep prayer. While many of us pray casually throughout the day—driving, possibly in the bathroom at work—there is a need for deeper, more focused prayer, as a part of our daily lives. While we explained how to pray in an earlier chapter, we must make a concerted, disciplined effort every day to focus entirely upon God in prayer. Our schedules are very busy and we have so many distractions, but we must be vigilant to ensure we have adequate time for God—not only to speak to Him but, more importantly, to listen to Him. Do you desire guidance? Do you want to stay on the right path toward your goals? You must make sure you are taking time to listen to God.

In Paul's excellent counsel in Ephesians 6, he talks about putting on spiritual armor. If you are a Christian and have spent any time in a church, you have likely heard a message or two about how to put on your spiritual armor. The scripture speaks for itself and has in mind the Roman soldier who typically wore specific items in order to prepare for battle. Do you realize that every day you wake up and your feet touch the floor you are engaged in a spiritual battle? Satan desires to render you useless for the kingdom of God. He wants you to be distracted and feel worthless and useless. His battleground is your mind, and he starts in on us from the moment we wake up in the morning. If you want to be victorious, if you want to look back over your life and be satisfied, then you must not only understand the schemes of the enemy, but prepare yourself to confront the enemy from the moment you awaken from sleep. I believe we are all creatures of habit, and one of the healthiest habits you can begin is mentally preparing yourself for every day as it begins.

Before your feet hit the floor, build a habit of putting on the helmet of salvation, asking God to protect your thoughts. Realize that the mind is the battleground of the enemy and is where he attacks you the most. Put on the breastplate of righteousness, reminding yourself that if you are a true believer you are forgiven and have been declared righteous by the blood of Jesus Christ. Remember throughout the day, when Satan tries to make you feel like a loser and as though you could never be forgiven, that your sins have been washed away! Put on the belt of truth, remembering to spend time in Scripture on a daily basis.

Tell yourself the truth; familiarize yourself with the truth so you know how to answer the enemy and so you can know the difference between truth and what the world, your workplace, television, etc., tell you. Have your feet fitted with the readiness that comes from the gospel of peace. Be prepared and ask God for opportunities to share your faith each day with everyone you can. Remember the shield of faith when you have difficulties that make you doubt. Put your faith in God, to believe His truths, to let the truths of scripture give you hope, peace, and confidence in Him. When the enemy shoots flaming arrows of discouragement that tempt you to quit, when fear makes you want to give in, when loneliness makes you despair, let faith in God protect you from stumbling. There is only one offensive weapon mentioned in Paul's description—the sword of the Spirit, which is the Word of God. I am in the process of building a habit of mentally putting on my armor every day. The days I remember are always better than those days I forget to wear it, and I believe it is an essential way of keeping me from being bludgeoned by the enemy on a daily basis.

How do you rank in spiritual swordplay? In wielding the sword of the spirit, are you a novice or a master? Two disciplines are critical in learning how to become a master swordsman, and a third can help us practice recalling scripture and improve our accountability. The first is the continual study of the God's Holy Scriptures. We must find a way to study daily, either through a study or reference Bible, an inductive approach, or well-respected commentaries. Most importantly, we must give ourselves ample time. You must find a way to carve out time in your daily schedule to spend time in the Word of God. Pray for direction, ask God to allow His Holy Spirit to lead you as you study, and make time to learn from Him through His Word. Having quiet time in God's Holy Word can be as simple as taking a notebook or a piece of paper, reading a few verses, and summarizing them in your own words, writing down the principles you see in numerical fashion. For example, in reading Psalms 119:1," Blessed are they whose ways are blameless, who walk according to the law of the LORD." you might find the principles:

1. We are blessed when we walk blamelessly.
2. We are blessed when we walk according to the law of God.

Upon finding principles, a quiet time is not complete without making them personal and applying them to your daily life:

1. Remember, I will be blessed today if I walk blamelessly.
2. Today, I will walk blamelessly.
3. Today, I will remember to follow God's law and walk according to it.

This is such a simple Bible study, but it is very profound and helpful in not only breaking down other, more difficult truths but applying them and helping them find practical application in our lives.

The second effective tool in becoming a master swordsman is memorizing scripture. Psalms tells us that David "hid God's Word" in his heart. How did Jesus confront Satan when He was tempted after fasting forty days and nights in Matthew? Each time Satan tempted Him, He responded with scripture (Matthew 4). Scripture is the answer, and every believer needs to do whatever possible to memorize scripture on a daily basis. An index card file with the days of the week would be a way to get started.

Take time to write a few verses on an index card with the scriptural reference included. Break each verse down into parts or take it verse by verse. Memorize each portion of the verse first, adding the next phrase or verse until you have mastered each scripture or scriptures. Take the index card with you throughout the day. Place it on the mirror in your bathroom or on the dash of your car. God will honor your commitment to memorizing His Word. Choose scriptures related to the issues with which you are dealing. Make them meaningful; you will find comfort, strength, and peace in difficult times and be better equipped to witness to others when you memorize God's Word.

The last spiritual disciple that bears mention is one that I believe many of us ignore often: witnessing. Are you witnessing to others? Are you sharing your spiritual lives with people you encounter daily? Jesus said that if we deny knowing Him before others He will deny us before our Father in heaven. Does that mean we need to stand on a street corner with a bullhorn while belting out the truth to others? Are we supposed to stand outside a grocery store and pass out tracts using "cold-turkey evangelism?" While that might be effective and a wonderful way to witness to others, one of the most effective ways is to turn everyday conversations toward spiritual matters.

If you can converse with another person, then you can witness to them by asking them questions about themselves. Most people will open up about their lives or whatever difficulties they have, and you can merely ask them if they would mind you praying for them. Sharing how God has brought you through certain situations or how your faith has helped you through specific difficulties, especially severe trials, can be very effective. Avoid using language that is only used in Christian circles, such as "saved, testify, the Word, prayed up, etc." We want to draw non-believers into the kingdom of God, not make becoming a believer some "unattainable," elusive goal.

Often, unbelievers already feel unworthy of God's love and feel as though God could never forgive them. This is what keeps many non-Christians from accepting Christ's free gift. How are we going to convince them salvation is free if we alienate them with our Christian lingo and forget to communicate the love of God? Am I saying people do not need to hear the truth? Absolutely not. Hell is real, and those who have not committed their lives to Christ are destined for eternity there. But we need to make sure we not only communicate the truth but ensure they understand the depth of God's grace, love, and mercy available to them.

The most effective way to win the lost is to build relationships, express our love to them, and model Christianity before them. Christ-like love is contagious, and others notice when we endure hardships with grace. Nothing exemplifies the power of God, nothing gives merit to the testimony of a believer like enduring, even, thriving in the midst of adversity. To become a powerful witness, we only need to intentionally build relationships with non-believers, showing their genuine love and concern, compassion, and grace. Additionally, if we want to witness to people we see in passing, we can do so by turning normal conversations toward Christ and by sharing something positive about our walk with God—or some struggle God has carried us through.

Sometimes we may be shocked by others' belief systems, behavior, or worldview. But why are we so surprised when unbelievers act…well…lost? We have to move beyond the self-righteous indignation and reach out to them. It is often those with the roughest edges, the most volatile, seemingly immature people who are the most ripe for the kingdom of God. Are you willing to see through the piercings, the tattoos, and the liberal mindset of others and build friendships with non-believers? No one is asking you to compromise your values and behave like them or lose your Christian faith for the sake of the lost, but it *does* mean we are responsible to do what we can to relate to them in a non-threatening, loving manner.

But remember, witnessing will improve your accountability quotient. If you begin mentioning the name of Jesus Christ, you will begin to examine yourself and how your life measures up to the Christian you are professing to be. Loving God and others means we use our resources wisely, devoting time and energy to discipline ourselves and grow as Christians.

IS GOD LIVING IN A GARBAGE CAN?

Do you care what you put into your body or whether or not your body gets regular exercise? Are you too busy or too broke to eat right and to be healthy? Loving yourself means taking care of your body.

How does exercise fit into the plan and will of God? Why should it matter that I take care of my body if it is only temporal? Not only are our bodies the temple of the Holy Spirit, there are many advantages to routine exercise as well. It can prevent disease, and coupled with healthy nutrition, can add many years to our lives. But there are other, more immediate benefits in addition to the spiritual aspects. Vigorous exercise releases endorphins, chemicals in our brain that produce pleasure. Did you know you can increase your level of happiness by exercising? While exercise is not always easy or fun, if we build habits that include regular exercise, we can lessen our tendency toward depression and reduce anxiety and stress as well—both of which lead to a healthier and longer life.

God desires for us to take care of His temple— His residence. We are stewards of our bodies, and exercise as well as healthy eating habits can not only help us live longer, but help us feel better along the way. I remember losing twenty-five pounds while experiencing some blood sugar issues, having decided to go on a diabetic diet. I weaned myself from sugars almost entirely, except for fruit, and tried to eat equal amounts of carbohydrates and proteins. I will never forget the way I felt, the surprisingly heightened energy level I experienced, and the fact that my mind seemed so much clearer. Now, after fifteen years of marriage and over fifty pounds gained, I am working toward becoming that fit again. Imagine walking around with a fifty-pound bag of sand on your shoulders everywhere you go. What a comfort it would be to drop that bag of sand and feel the incredible sense of relief, leaving those unwanted pounds behind!

Whatever your level of health, limitations, and lifestyle, all of us can do something to improve our health. Loving yourself means carving out some time to care for your body. Can you spare thirty minutes per day? Start improving your health today with a little bit of exercise and replacing something you are eating or drinking that isn't healthy. Try it one step at a time and see if you feel better. Jesus said "I came that you might have life, and have it abundantly" (John 10:10). Abundant life means a healthier life, one in which you maintain balance. Don't treat your body like a trash can, cramming unhealthy foods into it over and over again. Treat your body like the temple it should be.

ARE YOU A HURRICANE OR AN OCEAN BREEZE?

Is your life like a whirlwind? Do you have control of your life, or does it control you? Scripture says, "Be self-controlled and alert. Your enemy the devil prowls around like a roaring lion looking for someone to devour" (1 Peter 5:8). God wants you to be free to serve Him. Are you run-down? Do you feel as though you are burning the candle at both ends? Jesus completed His ministry in thirty-three years, and the most important aspects of His ministry were crammed into the last three years of His life. Was He tired? Absolutely. Did He desire for us to be so busy we would forget Him? Absolutely not! Jesus never burned out and never faded. He accomplished everything He set out to do, yet He always made time to worship and to find solace, especially when things were the most chaotic. He had to take a boat across a lake to get away from the crowds. He knew when He needed rest and when He needed peace and solitude. If Jesus needed rest, how much more do we?

Technology is so intertwined in our lives today that it gives us instant access to others. We are so connected that some of us rarely go five minutes without communicating with someone else. Some of us may feel guilty for even taking ten to fifteen minutes to be still and quiet. Our schedules are so full that when we have a moment, we feel compelled to use that time to check our messages or sit at the computer and send an e-mail—as though we would be unproductive to actually have ten minutes to think. Are you living that way? Is your schedule so busy you have no time for yourself? Or are you the type who cannot find the time to accomplish anything because you feel your life is so out of control?

"Busy-*ness*" can be a sign of a diligent person, but it can also create so much stress that it can be unhealthy. I must admit that time management, organization, and efficiency are things I struggle with constantly. On the continuum of structure, ranging between rigid organization and utter chaos, I fall dangerously close to the chaotic lifestyle. Of course, I could blame the fact that we have children with special needs and say that every plan I make gets changed, but how much more do special needs families need structure and organization? No matter what phase of life you find yourself in, diligence, organization, and structure are critical in becoming the person God wants you to be. Rarely will a day go by in which we accomplish everything we set out to do—there will always be changes, interruptions, and frustrations. But without attempting organization, without setting and focusing on goals, our lives pass by without incident devoid of accomplishing anything worthwhile.

One of the greatest differences I see between Jesus's day and ours is the fact that we have more distractions.

Phones equipped with Internet access can be a wonderful blessing when we need information, but they can also keep us from being aware of our surroundings, and cause us to disengage when we should be relating with people. The proliferation of cellular technology has brought many conveniences, but has also created a major problem with social interaction, not to mention distracting us while we continually check social media updates, e-mail, etc. It feels as though many of us are becoming adults with Attention Deficit, trying to coordinate electronic functions with actual human interaction, wrecking cars, disengaging from relationships, and missing opportunities to relate to our friends and family. The ultimate command encourages loving God and human beings, not our iPhones. We need to unplug from the electronic world for a day, a week, maybe a month, and reorganize our lives around devotion to God, rest, and awaken the spiritual dimension of our lives. Yes, it is easier said than done, but everyone, even people with heavy workloads, single parents, and those with busy lives, can restructure, regroup, simplify their lives, and make room for God. As God (through David) said, "Be still [cease striving] and know that I am God" (Psalms 46:10).

People are typically in one of two modes: they are either going nowhere, virtually spinning their wheels in the sand, or are too busy—sometimes a little of both. To those who seem to be circling the airport with nowhere to land—by all appearances drifting through life with little or no direction—I say seek God, His scripture, develop goals, and strive to be more diligent.

To those who feel they are caught up in hurricane force winds, pulled in every direction with too much on your plate, scrambling to put out fires in every area of your life, I say simplify your life. Look at your life, and where you are going. Take an hour, go for a drive somewhere, find some way to get alone with a pen and paper, a laptop, and look at your life goals. What do you want to accomplish? Write at least five areas of your life in which you want to set goals.

Goals need to be achievable and to be set carefully. Once goals have been set and you attempt to begin them, you may need to adjust them with your schedule. But remember, this system should be designed for you, and some of the goals ought to have a higher priority than others. I suggest ordering the list of goals so you can focus on those which are most important first. Be reasonable and remember that you are only one person and can only do so much. Maintain balance and learn to say no to yourself and to others when it is in your best interest to do so. The word "no" is very powerful, and you must be willing to eliminate the activities and commitments which hinder, distract, and create disorder in your life. Keep life as simple as possible, remembering to give yourself some flexibility, leisure, and down time. I realize this is next to impossible for some.

If you have special needs children, are a single parent, or are a very busy person, you may need to reach out to ask for help. Do not be afraid to ask; be willing to bless others by allowing them to help. Church families are wonderful places to build relationships with others with whom you can share the load. Parents need to carve out time for themselves as couples. Everyone needs time to get away, to find some way to regularly maintain time for yourself, and doing so requires a network of support from family and friends.

Most of us hate more than anything else to admit a need, but how else is the body of Christ going to have opportunities to serve without knowing the needs of others? Too often we try to go it alone, and we wonder why we are so frustrated, so callous, and feel so alone. We need each other, and until we are willing to reach out and to ask for help, we cause others to miss opportunities to bless us, to serve God, and receive the joy that comes from giving. Stop worrying about wearing out your welcome. No, life is not always pleasant, and we are not entitled to help from others, but how are we ever going to be helped unless we ask?

Balance is critical. Somewhere between being so rigid you cannot stop to talk to another or listen to the still small voice of God and having no structure, no system for maintaining diligence is a place of equilibrium. We need to find the place where we set goals, move toward them, and maintain some system of organization. We must manage our time and leave room for God to work, avoid walking in our own strength, and avoid being slaves to our schedules. We need to allow our schedules to help us maintain structure but have enough flexibility to build in time for God, time for our families, and time for ourselves. Such is the dilemma we will face for the rest of our lives. But to those who feel overwhelmed, I say take time for yourselves. You cannot be a good parent, a good worker, and more importantly, a good soldier for Christ by either being hapless and directionless or being too task-oriented. You must prevent yourself from being so inflexible, or so harried that you cannot take five minutes to pray or to take an opportunity to witness to, listen to, and speak with another. Work toward that equilibrium, keep trying to grow and find that place where you prevent burnout but are able to maximize your potential.

BALANCING LOVE WITH BOUNDARIES

Just as balance is required in our personal lives, we need to learn to love others without taking the weight of the world on our shoulders. I have noticed, in my home in the southern half of the United States and specifically in the church at large, most are gracious, hospitable, typically avoid conflict, and want to get along with others. It is a wonderful blessing to live in such a place where peace abounds and where people at least attempt to be friendly and care for one another. Unfortunately, within the church in the deep south and anywhere people connect, a natural byproduct of our Christian culture is a tendency for some to be people-pleasers. People pleasers fear conflict, dread disappointment from others, and feel incapable of saying no. For those who have difficulty with conflict, saying no is more than uncomfortable; it is loathsome business that creates nervousness, anxiety, and sometimes sheer terror. These individuals often have difficulty knowing where their responsibilities end and where another person's begins. They often wonder, "Where do I draw the line?"

For example, Julie's mother continuously interferes with her marriage, interjecting her opinions without being asked, insulting Julie's husband, and causing disturbances and discomfort during family events. Blood, however, is thicker than water, and Julie makes excuses for her mother. "She is just lonely and misses Daddy since he died," Julie explains, "but she will grow and get better over time." Her husband is left feeling powerless and is unable to fix the situation and withdraws—hurt and angry by this abrasive person who refuses to go away. He knows it is Julie's place to go to bat for him and to confront her mother and establish a healthy boundary. Deep down, Julie wants to feel as though she and her husband were an independent family, but she is scared to death of the prospect of hurting her mother's feelings. So Julie continues to be the go-between, trying to keep peace between herself and her mother while feeling trapped under the weight and pressure of the situation, unable to fix the problem.

In another example, Rachel feels overwhelmed and constantly berated by her boss who is never pleased. While working overtime on the weekends and being constantly pulled in every direction, she feels as though she might crack at any moment. She is having trouble balancing the pressure and responsibility of work, church responsibilities, and her home life. People at church are looking to her to organize Vacation Bible School, direct the choir for the homecoming service next month, and somehow manage to carve out enough time to get her children to morning camp and art classes. "How am I going to handle all this?" she muses. "If I don't do it, who will?" Rachel cannot say no, even though she is running out of emotional and physical energy trying to keep up with everything.

Dave has been married for thirty-one years. His wife Sara is precious, and they have two beautiful children, twenty-five-year-old Greg and twenty-nine-year-old Mark. Mark is responsible, hard-working, and successful, having put himself through college and begun working creating accounting software. Greg, on the other hand, seems to lack focus. He has recently moved back home and was just let go from his job for missing too many days. He is tired of his life and has very little motivation. Dave wants desperately to help his son grow up and longs for him to find his niche but is afraid to tell him the truth for fear of his sensitive nature. He knows Greg needs to be on his own by now, but he just can't seem to find the right way to tell him. "What if I tell him the truth and he spirals into depression?" Dave asks.

These are examples of unhealthy boundaries and people for whom saying no is too uncomfortable. Rather than say what needs to be said, biting the bullet, and confronting the issue, these people are willing to endure the pain and remain in a constant state of discomfort to avoid drawing the line. How liberating it would be to take a stand, to say no! To understand boundaries one must contemplate where his responsibility ends and where another's responsibility begins.

What happens, you may ask, when my coworker gives me a guilt trip for telling her no? What if my sister never wants to speak with me again when I tell her

I want to spend Christmas with my immediate family? Who will take care of the church social, the little league snacks, and the vacation Bible school if I'm not helping? Are you compelled to say yes to everything? Stop! There is nothing wrong with being busy for the kingdom of God in your community or at work as long as these are activities you choose and those you decide you have energy to do. God gives us so many resources, and it is up to us to determine where they are best used. A good steward manages not only the financial resources God gives, but time and energy as well. Prioritize, plan, and make the best use of your time. Do not let others choose what you will do; make your own choices based upon what God would have you do.

If you want to establish healthy boundaries and if you are ready to extricate yourself from the bonds—the slavery of having to please everyone around you—then take some time and sit down with a pen and paper. Consider the most important situations and relationships in which you feel trapped. Think through them, taking time to see where you have been given more responsibility than what should rightfully be yours. List the different people or groups with whom you associate. List the situations, the conflicts, and the places where you feel you have been unfairly treated, taken advantage of, and made to feel responsible for that which you shouldn't.

In each situation, each relationship, one at a time, think through where each went wrong and where you could have responded differently. One at a time, little by little, you must create change. You cannot correct others' dependence upon you, and you cannot make them learn to respect your boundaries. You can, however, change how you respond and how you relate. The burden placed upon you by others is yours to either keep bearing or hand back to them. The choice is yours.

Determine in your mind that you will make change, and you will find opportunities to establish boundaries in your life. Think of an upcoming situation, at work, with your extended or immediate family, or with a friend or group. Decide how you will respond differently next time, praying for God's guidance. In each situation, play it through in your mind or write down your response—what you have decided needs to happen to initiate change. Find an opportunity to practice this concept of establishing boundaries. This is the critical moment of your life where you can either choose to grow, choose to take action, or keep nodding in agreement with this information and go on suffering. Will you act? Will you go in the courage of God's spirit and free yourself from this burden? Change requires action; it is something you do, not something with which you merely agree. Do you need support to make this happen? Find it. Do you need a counselor, a pastor, or a friend to walk you through these critical changes in your life to help you be accountable? Find one. You must take the first step.

After you have made an effort to establish a healthy boundary with someone, you will often find that the person doesn't understand. They may continue to have unhealthy expectations of you and may continue to cross the line you have set. Just as the unhealthy pat-

THOMAS C. BATES, M.S.

terns have taken time—often years to develop—it may take several attempts to re-establish them and time for others to realize you mean business. Saying no without feeling guilty is a very difficult thing to do, but it can be very liberating! Once you realize you need to work on this area of your life, look for opportunities to assert yourself—as uncomfortable as it may seem at first. Give yourself credit when you are successful, focus on making deliberate effort in making a change. Take some time to feel the release and the freedom you gain from taking charge of your life from making your own choices. Realize the joy that comes from choosing to engage in; commit to only the things that you have the energy, the resources, and the time to do. Saying no can be the first step in re-ordering your life, simplifying your schedule, and making life manageable again. Only you can cut the strings, and only you can, with God's help, affect change in your life.

MAKING THE MOST OF SINGLE LIVING

As one who remained single for ten years out of high school after becoming heartbroken over a relationship, I am familiar with the joys and pains of single adulthood. I have felt the pain and loneliness of singleness, but I have also seen God work in miraculous ways during that time in my life. Singleness is a gift, and while marriage and parenting are beautiful and rewarding, having the ability to be singly devoted to God is not without its merits and pleasures, as well. Are you single? Are you lonely? Do you long for a mate, wondering if you will ever find the right person for you? You must consider whether or not you believe God is sovereign or whether He is truly in control to find contentment in your singleness.

If you do believe God is in charge, then regardless of your emotions, you must admit that God has a plan for you and that He desires for you to be content, happy, and satisfied in Him alone. While marriage may be in your future, the possibility exists that it may not. Regardless, you must seek Him, seek the Scriptures, search your heart, and move accordingly.

There is no place in your life for self-pity, false guilt that says you do not deserve happiness, or feelings of worthlessness that stand against the value God has placed on your life. You are on a path, whether or not it is the right path depends upon your relationship with Jesus Christ and your willingness to be obedient to His Holy Scriptures. As a single adult, you are in a wonderful position of great possibility in which Paul said, "Now to the unmarried and the widows I say: It is good for them to stay unmarried, as I am [unmarried]" (1 Corinthians 7:8). Why would he say that when marriage is obviously God's mandate for Adam and Eve and the rest of the world to multiply and fill the earth? Single adults are in a unique position to do great exploits for the kingdom of God. The closest I have ever been to God was during my twenties as a single adult. Make the most of this time in your life while you are able to be devoted to God without the distractions of family responsibilities.

Does this mean you should desire singleness and avoid searching for a mate? Of course not, unless you feel God would have you be single. There is nothing wrong with dating, continuing to seek, or "[casting] your bread upon the waters" (Ecclesiastes 11:1). How else will you know whether God desires marriage for your life unless you try to seek companionship? You must seek balance between burying your head in the sand, living as a recluse or desperately throwing yourself at anyone with a pulse.

As a man, I am unfamiliar with the longings women have for bearing children, so I do not want to make light of the deep desire many feel to marry and begin a family before the biological clock stops ticking. But I truly believe it is better to be lonely and to do without than it is to make unwise, hasty decisions about marriage. Finding a life mate, in my opinion, is a critical decision and is second only to making a decision to give your life to Christ. Much care and consideration should come before choosing a life partner. How many decisions about marriage have been made without the proper contemplation, and couples wound up in divorce with grievous consequences? On the scale of traumatic and stressful events, divorce is second only to the death of a spouse or child. Endeavor in your heart to make your choice for a life mate carefully, and have every intention of making it last for life.

How do you go about looking for a mate? There are many choices and many methods, including online dating services, speed-dating, single adult ministries, and meeting people through friends. One of the healthiest ways to get to know someone is through group dating where you are able to meet and talk in a safe, casual setting without the intensity of a one-on-one meeting.

As a youth pastor and high school teacher, I have seen the awkwardness of teens as they make attempts at conversation with the opposite sex. I have often referred to one of the wonderful pieces of wisdom offered by Jim Dobson to teenagers regarding learning to converse with others. He said we can approach conversation like a friendly game of tennis—not competing with another but simply hitting the ball back and forth. When we ask a simple question like, "Where are you from?" it is much like hitting the ball over the net to the other person. If they answer, "I am from Dalton, Georgia," you might ask another question, "Tell me about your family," and you've kept the ball in play. Keeping the conversation going can give you an opportunity to get to know another person, and the more comfortable you become asking deeper questions, the better you will know them. Dating is a pre-requisite to marriage, and the more you understand a potential life mate, the happier you will be in a relationship with them. Understanding a person is paramount in ensuring you will be compatible with them and capable of making a marriage not only last but thrive, and you will be in a much better position to enjoy the union when you have taken the time to know them fully.

Many couples begin marriage with a great deal of baggage such as trust issues, insecurities, and half-hearted commitment. They often wear blinders, overlooking each other's faults while dating and wind up dazed and confused years later in marriage. Time and time again, radio counseling programs are filled with disgruntled individuals who wake up a few years after marriage to find a stranger in their bed. "When we were dating, he bought me flowers, went to church with me, prayed with me, and loved my extended family. Now it feels like I am married to a different person. My dreams of the perfect marriage are shattered." What happened between the dating relationship and the post-honeymoon bliss?

Couples always put their best foot forward and shine their vehicles, their shoes, and themselves while dating.

Women wear their most alluring clothes, perfect their make-up, say all the right things, and men do likewise. Why do we do this? All our efforts, unconsciously, go into doing what we can to win the love of our life. There is a sort of *aura* around couples in the dating mode—a glow that can blind us from reality. Unless we make a sincere effort to remain sober-minded while searching for a mate and while getting to know the person we are dating, we can cause a great deal of heartache and wasted time moving in the wrong direction.

Happy couples learn to communicate before becoming engaged and before getting married, and they discuss important issues and ensure compatibility regarding values, life goals, and personalities before tying the knot. Marriages today are often made with haste and with the idea that marriage is just a contract we can tear up if we don't like each other. But, the pain and heartache can be avoided if we can approach marriage with the utmost care. While our heart must be somewhat vulnerable to opening ourselves emotionally to another, we must not neglect using our head, thinking through our decisions. A healthy individual will find the balance between allowing his heart to be open, taking an emotional risk by investing time and feelings toward another, and taking a somewhat scientific approach to understanding the other person.

Getting to know your partner's family background, upbringing, and how they handle conflict and emotion is important. Does your partner want children? How do they plan to discipline them? Do they want two children or twenty-three? Are your partner's parents willing to release their child? Will there be conflicts in "leaving and cleaving?" Was your partner spoiled, neglected, forced into adulthood early or allowed to be lazy? Is your partner selfish? All of these questions are vital in knowing who they are and in seeing past the superficial shell we place around ourselves while dating. Once you are aware of your partner's misgivings, are you willing to deal with that for the rest of your life? If so, then you better be prepared because anyone who is married will tell you the little idiosyncrasies you dislike will become amplified and will likely never change after marriage. If you have the notion that you will be able to change your partner and help mold them into the person you want them to be, please be forewarned; only God Himself can change your mate—not you!

While you are dating someone, understand that you will go through various levels of commitment—from knowing them and being able to trust them, becoming exclusive as a couple, and finally becoming engaged. It takes time to get to know another person. Love at first sight may happen, but I have counseled many couples who said they no longer felt love for one another. Feelings of love ebb and flow, and commitment is the key to a lasting relationship—gutting it out when you feel like giving up. Do not hesitate to ask your partner about their level of commitment. If they are not willing to move forward, you should be prepared for that possibility.

Remember that relationships are not the recipe for contentment. By all means, remember this phrase— "Two emotional halves do not make a whole!" If you are looking for that person who will complete you and who will satisfy your every need, beware—there is no such person. Relationships, like marriage, are about giving, not taking. Mature love is not selfish but is willing to give when you will at times receive nothing in return. With that, I would add this; you are ready for marriage when you reach the point of spiritual maturity where you would be perfectly content to be united with Christ without a mate for the rest of your life. Then and only then are you ready for someone to come alongside you to join you in your journey. Unless you are willing to say that honestly and to sincerely live that way, you are not ready to be married. Marriage will not solve all your problems; in many cases, it will increase them. Marriage is precious, and it is sacred and full of joy, but it is also very, very hard work. Relationships are not to be a security blanket, and seeking another for fear of being alone is not only unhealthy but possibly dangerous. Relationships should be entered into with caution; as well, they are not meant to be treated with casual indifference, especially when couples are considering them serious enough to live together.

Many feel that the healthiest thing one can do is to live together before marriage. It gives the couple, they believe, an opportunity to have a test run at marriage. Unfortunately, evidence suggests that living together and becoming sexually active before marriage can actually reduce marital satisfaction. Many women wait years for their male partners to propose marriage while living together.

Some say marriage is obsolete, but I beg to differ. I recently counseled a couple who constantly had difficulty with resolving problems. They had both been married and divorced and were hesitant to get married from having been burned. Having lived together for five years, they were contemplating marriage. Unfortunately, their arguments constantly escalated into meltdowns, and they had difficulty resolving even the mildest of issues.

During their arguments, one or the other typically mentioned the fact that they didn't have to stay in this relationship but may as well leave. I reached an impasse with them and finally had to tell them that I could help them with communication and to build trust, but the one thing they lacked was commitment. Without the commitment of marriage, the covenant which says before God that we purpose to stay together forever, relationships often fail. No counselor in the world can make a couple be committed—either they are or are not. Living together may seem like the best course, but it often is a symptom of a lack of commitment rather than a spurning of the concept of marriage. Either way, until couples understand the value of Christ-honoring marriage, they will typically find themselves unhappy and unfulfilled.

In addition, many believe that aside from living together, becoming physically intimate is a way to test the compatibility of a relationship. If they have no secrets from each other and are able to become intimate before getting married, they will know whether or not they will be satisfied with one another for life. In speaking with couples who remained pure—yes, there are couples who have done so—they have absolutely no regrets with avoiding intimacy until becoming married. As archaic as that might seem to those reading this book, couples who *do* remain pure actually find themselves more satisfied. There is a sense of discovery and a lack of guilt that continues throughout their lives.

In addition to marital satisfaction by remaining pure before marriage, there are other factors worthy of consideration. Statistics prove that one in three adults now are affected by some form of sexually transmitted disease. Those facts are staggering. Imagine that for every three people you date, one will likely have an issue. That in itself is a reason to take your time before becoming intimate with someone you date.

If that is not enough to give you pause, more than any other concern, one should consider matters of the heart before physically tying the knot. When you become one with another physically, it produces a false sense of intimacy. Engaging in sexual behavior takes the relationship exponentially to the next level. Expectations change, couples often feel as though they are married, and breaking the relationship hurts much more deeply. Just as it is wretchedly painful to pry apart one's fingers after super-gluing them together, the heart is shattered when couples who have become intimate separate. Becoming one has consequences, and when you break, a part of you stays behind with that partner.

Singles must be very careful with these powerful urges. Only with marriage is this fire meant to burn. Without the sanctity of marriage, pressure, guilt, and anxiety will accompany sexual behavior. Ask yourself this question, "Am I worth waiting for until marriage?" Even in this modern age, any man worth your time will wait for you. If he is not willing, he does not deserve you. Make up your mind how far you are willing to go and adamantly proclaim this to those you plan to date. If they pressure you or try to woo you, stick to your guns, and you will find the man worth waiting for will honor your wishes.

Enjoy your singleness while you are in this phase of your life and make the most of this time. For many, much of the journey is spent longing for the next phase of life. In elementary school, we long for high school; in high school, we long to graduate. After we finish one stage and move on to another, how many of us wish we could go back and do it over again, making better decisions. Enjoy the journey and enjoy your youth. If you are single again through divorce or the death of a spouse, do not waste your energy upon loneliness and regret; instead, use the resources you have toward happiness, joy, and peace. Do not allow the pain of heartbreak to consume you and to sap you of the energy you could be using in the service of God.

Being single is not a curse, it is a huge blessing. How much greater can you love God and others, when you are able to focus completely on them as a single adult? This is not a time for sadness or loneliness, but a time for reflection, for working on who you are, or who you want to be. Allow God to help you become a deeper person. Take time to cultivate relationships and test the waters, to refine your relationship skills while dating.

Use this time to serve God, serve the church, travel, save your money, and develop self-discipline. Trust me, when you become married, you will need these time-worn habits like managing and saving your money and developing spiritual disciplines so you can carry them into marriage. This is a perfect time to read and develop communication skills, learning how to be a husband or wife or parent. It is not a sin to plan and prepare with expectations of becoming married or having children, in fact it is wise. Contemplate how many children you want, what your life goals are, and the standard of living you desire. Pray and seek God continually for direction, but do not allow these prayers to cause you to be desperate. Never allow fear to drive you to making a wrong choice for a partner in the most sacred relationship of marriage.

Should God decide for you to be single for life, do not fret or fear, be satisfied and content with Him. Live in the knowledge that yours will be a life filled with devotion, service, and joy. Find your gifts, engage in them, and live. Do not allow the well-meaning intentions of others, in their desire to see you married to cause you pain. Consider it your duty to teach them that singleness is God's gift, however long it lasts, to provide opportunities for crowns to lay at His feet when your life is over.

OUR SWAN SONG— LOVING OUR MATE

Why is it that the most important relationship, other than our relationship with Christ, often suffers the most? Why does our spouse often get the leftovers in our lives? Like many other areas in our lives, busy-*ness* often creates problems in our marriages. We focus on work, on children, and on other responsibilities, and so many things can push away our wives and husbands— and *they* get left out in the cold. Past hurts, baggage from previous relationships, discomfort in relating to others, or bitterness from emotional injuries within the marriage can cause a disconnect between partners. There is a reason many vows contain "what God hath joined together, let no man put asunder" (Matthew 19:6). There are much more than *Fifty Ways to Leave your Lover* and even more ways in which the enemy attacks our marriage relationships. If the devil can destroy a marriage, he can wreak havoc on the children and on our whole society. America is filled with homes that have been split in divorce. Counseling centers all over the nation are filled with parents, step-parents, and children suffering from rejection, pressure, chaos, depression, and pain as a result of broken marriages.

Among other patterns, in my practice as a counselor, I have seen two ever-present themes. Husbands are often in complete denial, completely tuned out, apathetic, and clueless that there is a problem within their marriage in the first place; conversely, wives are typically aware much sooner that their marriage is in jeopardy, and their pleas for help go unnoticed. They often feel helpless to create change or feel as though they have blown it with their choice of a marriage partner. "Maybe I'll do better next time," they lament. Rather than fighting to save their marriage and working toward enhancing and holding their husbands accountable, they want an easy way out of their circumstances. What they do not realize is that the stress, emotional and financial pressure, guilt, isolation, and chaos they feel after the divorce are often far worse than the mediocre marriage they experienced while it remained. There are opportunities to mend hurting relationships, and they are worth trying to restore before ending them abruptly without an effort to do so.

Sometimes separation is the healthiest method of dealing with a situation, but only when it is absolutely necessary. Whenever there is an opportunity, encouraging healthy communication between your spouse and his or her peers who support your marriage is beneficial. Regardless, counseling is very important in preventing marriage collapse, as well being as a deterrent to divorce in the midst of problems. When you are sick, you go to the doctor to get well. When your vehicle needs repair, you go to a mechanic to get advice or fix the automobile. Why is it that we avoid counseling like the plague? Why do we feel stigmatized when we consider going to a specialist to help with relationship problems? We need to remember that just like there are shoddy mechanics who take us to the cleaners, there are counselors who do not share our value systems and who can be unhealthy sources of information. Just as you would shop around for a good mechanic or a good pediatrician, it is important to ask trusted individuals and be willing to ask pertinent questions regarding your counselor's values. Remember, you are free to end a counseling relationship if you do not feel there is a good fit with your personality, or conflicts with regard to your values.

Just as you need routine maintenance to keep a vehicle running properly to prolong its life, you need to maintain your marriage to not only stay together, but to enjoy your relationship together. Healthy couples communicate well, work together to solve problems, share life goals, place the marriage covenant in high esteem, are in agreement with regard to role expectations and values, and spend quality time together not only as a family, but as a couple. Healthy couples have activities they enjoy together.

Sometimes compromise is in order, such as a wife who takes up hunting or a husband who learns to enjoy going to yard sales with his wife. Husbands and wives need to communicate commitment, to let each other know, especially during the difficult times, that they are in it for the long haul. Husbands need to make marriage a priority, and wives need to do the same, putting everything aside, at times, to ensure each is important to the other. Marriage should be more important than work, more than activities, and even more than a couple's children. Marriage should be first under our personal relationship with Christ, and neglecting each other can not only create problems elsewhere in life but cause the eventual erosion of the relationship.

Healthy marriages possess skills for handling problems. They don't avoid problems and suffer in silence resenting one another, but instead are willing to share and face issues. Typically in relationships, there are *runners* and *chasers*. Runners want to avoid conflict or need time to sort through their feelings. They feel uncomfortable at the mere thought of disagreements and do whatever they can to avoid it. Chasers, on the other hand, cannot rest until they can fix what is wrong. They feel uncomfortable when things are not right between them and their partner. They will chase down and bug the other person and even create a different conflict just to get to the bottom of the original problem. Runners need space and a "cool down" period to think the issue through while chasers need to know that their partner is willing to deal with the issue. The healthiest solution is for couples to have ground rules when one is upset with the other. One wise counselor explained that when he and his wife were in conflict, he (the chaser) would let his wife know that he would be at the kitchen table in thirty minutes to discuss the issue. He will wait patiently for his wife to meet him at the table, and if she is ready, she will join him. If not, he tries again after a period of time.

For some couples, giving the runner ten or fifteen minutes is enough to satisfy the need to process their feelings. Some couples feel that the scripture which states, "Do not let the sun go down while you are angry" means they literally cannot sleep without solving the problem, immediately (Ephesians 4:26). Others believe that, as a couple, they need to come to the point where they have at least agreed to disagree, without resentment before turning in to bed. This can be a difficult subject since many arguments result from being exhausted when emotions can be high and our minds are less capable of rational thinking. I have heard of an acronym using the word "HALT" to help remember when care should be taken before resolving conflict. We should be very careful or even postpone discussing a problem when either of us is H-hungry, A-angry, L-lonely or T-tired. While we cannot completely avoid problems we should be careful of our respective emotions before considering solving a problem. Regardless, conflicts need to be resolved in a reasonable amount of time—hopefully within twenty-four hours or sooner, if possible.

Problem solving is important, but the method of working through conflict is equally important. Men and women, despite efforts to prove otherwise, are very different in their approach to life, relationships, and solving problems. Human beings have three essential elements, and function in three different ways: *thinking*, *feeling*, and *doing/behaving*. If we think of these elements as three cars in a train, they will be aligned differently for men and women.

Men often have the "doing" car up front and the "thinking" car behind it, but the "feeling" car is somewhere down the track, derailed or lagging way behind. Why do men have trouble identifying, owning, and understanding feelings? While there are exceptions to this rule, men typically grow up being taught that crying and admitting they cannot handle a problem is unacceptable—that expressing feeling is a sign of weakness. What do mothers often do on the playground when a girl falls? They might say, "Poor baby," pick her up, and nurture her. But when a boy falls, they often take care of him differently. A dad might say, "Rub some dirt on it, and it'll be all right!" As a result, the only socially acceptable emotion for men to express is anger. Men have to be taught that they can be men and still have feelings, and understanding them, owning them, communicating them will help them enhance their relationships and make them better men. Women, on the other hand, will often have the feeling car up front, pulling the train. They could benefit from realizing while they are gifted at intuition, at understanding, and recognizing feelings and expressing them, they need not be ruled by—often yanked around by—their emotions.

When the thinking car is up front, we are able to make healthy decisions, relate to others better, and avoid the derailments of quarrels that hurt others, not to mention blow-ups that result in missed opportunities to solve problems and often lead to resentment and bitterness. Both men and women can benefit from thinking first, feeling second, and behaving after having thought through their feelings.

Problem solving requires effective communication. Effective communication involves someone speaking, and someone listening. Paula Ortwein, in her excellent *Mastering the Mysteries of Love* curriculum, teaches couples to show understanding and to put yourself in your partner's shoes while listening (Ortwein 6-14-11).[6] Simply put, listening effectively involves turning off your own agenda and focusing completely upon your partner, especially when you are mad and you want to dominate the conversation. Good listeners can quench the fire of conflict quickly by turning off the television, showing with your body that you are listening by facing your partner and honing in on what they are saying and remembering the *gist* of what they have said—trying to focus on what they are feeling.

Once you have heard your partner, say what you believe they are feeling back to them. For example, if your wife says, "My boss chewed me out today in front of all my coworkers!" You could respond, "It sounds like you felt very embarrassed, maybe even humiliated by the way he chose to do that in front of everyone." Notice the husband focused on what he believed his wife was feeling—embarrassed—rather than just the facts. When a partner can hone in on what his partner felt, he is better able to understand her and really step inside her shoes. When you feel heard and when you feel understood, you feel validated, as though you are important to your partner. Couples must remember that if an issue is important to their partner, no matter how insignificant it might seem to them, it should be important and worthy of listening to.

Effective communication requires not only listening but skillful expression of what you have to say. Many can speak, but few do so effectively. Women and men need to know that how they speak—the delivery of their message—is critical. Delivery is the key to whether or not the information will be received. She can shout and she can scream until she is blue in the face, but as long as her partner's defenses are up, her message will fall upon deaf ears. What happens when we feel someone is condescending and when we feel disrespected by another? We either become passive-aggressive and find a back door to get what we want, or we blow up and retaliate. Effective speakers think about what they need to say beforehand, setting up the situation for success. They start with something positive, trying to find the good in their partner's intentions. For example, if you want your husband to help you clean, you might say, "Jimmy, I know you have worked hard all day, and I'm very grateful for all you have done at your job, but if you can help me do these dishes, I will have more time and energy to devote to you tonight." Maintain respect for each other and find out what sets your partner off, avoid pushing their buttons and causing their defenses to go up, and you will be much more likely to find success at having your needs met.

Young couples often have no clue how to discuss problems and will often avoid situations to prevent conflict. When my wife and I had been married for six months or so, I was serving bi-vocationally as a youth pastor. At our church, there was a part German Shepherd dog who came to visit every Sunday. Week after week, my wife Jessica would say, "Aww, look at that dog! We should take it home!" Finally, we agreed to take the dog to our small rental home.

Soon afterward, the dog was in heat and attracted the neighborhood male dogs, and to our horror, in the competition our next door neighbor's older dog was killed in the fray, causing our neighbors to consider us their enemy. As you can imagine, our dog became pregnant and proceeded to give birth to six puppies—five of which survived. Winter arrived, and though I had built a doghouse and pen outside, Jessica begged me to allow the puppies to be brought indoors. Like many honeymooner husbands, I complied. Soon, the carpet in one of our closets was shredded, and the kitchen floor was covered in puppy droppings. At this point, Jessica was expecting our first child, and I wouldn't dare have her on her hands and knees scrubbing the floor. So there I was, Cinderella-style, on my knees, cleaning, contemplating the repairs, the cleaning, and the fear of losing our deposit on our rental home, all because I avoided confronting a problem!

Healthy couples are willing to discuss problems, are creative in finding solutions, and have a place in their relationship where they can not only identify improvements but work together to accomplish them. Just as a business requires growth, learning, and implementing new systems, marriage requires flexibility, willingness to change, and hard work to achieve it. Emotions can often be high, and couples need to learn to talk through their feelings and get them out in the open to avoid building up resentment and bitterness.

If the person who is the most frustrated is given an opportunity to talk, and the partner who is in better control of his emotions is willing to listen, couples can work through issues more smoothly and avoid eruptions and escalating tempers. Couples need a plan to take a time out if they are too frustrated to talk but be willing to resume the conversation when they have calmed down. Respect is critical in heated conversations and avoiding comparisons, bringing up the past and pushing buttons is imperative in reducing conflict.

Working through disagreements is essential to maintain a healthy relationship, but it takes practice and time, willingness to engage, and unselfish love to be successful. Discussing and solving problems without temper tantrums, without blowing up is an art, and couples must practice it to get better over time. Maybe you have a problem that just isn't going away. In your mind, you think, "I've talked to him over and over, and he just doesn't care. But your resentment, your frustration, is evident. Something isn't right, and nothing you do seems to overcome the issue. Be creative, try to honestly put yourself in your partner's shoes, and understand his perspective.

Sometimes there are problems that you will never be able to solve, and you have to decide whether or not it is a deal breaker. When you say "I do," there are always going to be issues that are part of the entire deal. Only you can decide if this is something you can live with or not. Remember, you cannot change your partner—only God can. You can create an environment, however, in which your husband or wife can better achieve change.

If you want your husband to help you clean, cook, help with the children, unless it is a matter of life and death, avoid scrutinizing his every effort. Catch him doing something helpful, something positive, and praise him for it. Here are some scenarios of difficulties I have encountered in counseling.

John is remarried, and his wife Kim is frustrated because John's children from a previous marriage have no boundaries when they come to their house. John's ex-wife Julie is no better, and every time John's kids come home from their mother's house, they have to be re-oriented to the new rules. Chaos abounds, and Kim feels as though she is going insane with absolutely no control over her step-children.

John wants his children to feel comfortable when they are home. He knows they have been forced to adapt to this new situation. "They didn't ask to be split between two homes," he explains, and guilt drives him to be lenient with them. Children know how to manipulate situations and will often play parents against each other to create a comfortable *rule-free* environment for themselves. Children of divorce always suffer, either by a lack of boundaries and consequences, or by being placed in the middle as spies while ex-spouses battle in co-parenting situations. How many fatherless children suffer from a lack of positive male influences in their lives? All over the world, families are ripped apart by divorce, and society reels from the wake of its impact.

John and Kim need counseling, and John must be willing to put aside the guilt which is driving him to be lenient with the children and develop boundaries and structure for the children. While in John's home, the children must understand that these are the expectations, and consequences must be consistently enforced. It is John's responsibility, as the blood parent of the children to take the lead with regard to discipline, and he must have a united front with Kim. Kim must realize that this was a package deal, and she cannot control what happens with the children, within reason, while they are at their mother's home. Kim needs reassurance that she will not be disrespected, and it is John's responsibility to step up and be their father. These situations are all too common in America today, and much care is needed in resolving these co-parenting situations.

Family is critical, marriage is sacred, and we have moved so far away from God's intended design that the result is devastating. What is the solution? Should anyone who has been divorced go back to their original partner, forsaking their current marriage and reconciling with their initial mate? Unfortunately, it is not that simple. Yes, God hates divorce, and His intention has always been one partner for life. God made provision for divorce only in situations where there was adultery.

But regardless, as with other perversions of God's intentions, the results cause grievous and painful consequences. "Are you telling me if my husband is beating me I should stick it out?" No, when you are in an unsafe situation, you must remove yourself from the danger. But reconciliation is biblical, and whenever possible it is the healthiest route. Restoration is clearly the best alternative, but both partners must be willing to change and willing to focus on their own individual issues rather than pointing blame at the other spouse.

Offenders must be willing to fully acknowledge their own faults, and those who have been offended must see true repentance, a willingness on the offender's part to show consistent behavioral change over time. Old behavior patterns are hard to change, but change is possible with the right accountability, much effort, and most importantly, God's intervention.

In abusive situations, the offender typically has issues of control. A husband feels he cannot control his wife, so he verbally or physically abuses her. While this is not always the case, it often happens this way. While the saying is true that opposites attract, an aggressive person mixed with a passive partner typically results in a very harmful situation. Patterns of control are very hard to break, and unless there is serious divine intervention and consistent real change over a long period of time, controllers will never change. Many controllers and/or abusers operate in a cycle. Frustrations over lack of control or other issues result in abuse, after which the abuser feels remorseful. Remorse causes the abuser to behave appropriately, even apologetically, and things return to normal for a time until some other situation causes the abuser to become frustrated again and perpetrate abuse—and the cycle continues.

Abusers often pair up with those who are passive, who may need rescuing, or may have grown up in homes where they were given very little freedom or ability to make choices. Passive people often look for someone to parent them, make decisions for them, and take care of them. They gravitate toward people who are strong and easily become dependent upon their spouse or partner. When abuse happens, they feel powerless and unable to extricate themselves from the situation as though there are no alternatives for them. They often feel financially dependent, lack confidence in their ability to go at it alone, and feel they are better off taking their chances with an abuser than making a change. The results can often be catastrophic, and victims of abuse will often go through cycles of leaving, returning, and leaving again, risking their life as well as the lives of their children as they return to these dangerous situations. While healthy marriages should keep no secrets, in cases of abuse, the victim must be willing to formulate a plan of escape—packing a bag of clothing with the number for a shelter or center for abuse and setting aside enough money for transportation. Whatever it takes, victims must find a way to separate themselves from their abuser to ensure their safety as well as for their children.

There is a vast difference between biblical, male, servant leadership and a man exerting power over a woman. A servant leader does just that—he serves. He creates an environment for his wife so that she flourishes and so she feels special, cared for, and emotionally nurtured where her needs are met. A servant leader does not need to engage in power struggles; he is too busy helping her in the kitchen! A wife who is healthy emotionally, who is being served by her husband, need not feel inferior, or feel the need to exert her power. She feels the contentment from being served, and in returning the favor is so busy caring for her husband that she does not fear being dominated. She is too satisfied to need to exert her solidarity. Roles have tended to change in this society, and the need for income has driven many couples to require two incomes to survive. While having husbands and wives working full-time is not the best scenario for couples with children, it is often necessary.

The ideal situation is to have one parent home to care for the children. But speaking from someone who has tried to survive on less than thirty thousand dollars of annual income in America with a family of six, the reality is that having one income is very difficult, to say the least. Much care and consideration is needed to do whatever one can to make provisions for caring for a child's emotional needs.

We need to provide positive interaction with our children and do whatever we can to avoid burnout and having daycares or televisions raise our children. Times are tough, but we need a support system like the church to help ensure our children get all they need to thrive. Single parents and parents of special needs children are the most vulnerable to burnout, and churches and other organizations need to step up to give them respite and emotional support. It is very true that we cannot parent effectively if we are not caring for our own individual needs and our needs as a couple.

Kasey recently found some illicit material on her husband Don's computer. They have been married for seventeen years, and she has never suspected any problems with pornography. Digging deeper, she finds websites he has spent their money visiting, and she feels the sting of betrayal and is as crushed as if he had an affair with another woman. When confronted, Don tries to make light of the situation, assuring her it is nothing. Kasey is furious and is ready to find an attorney to end their marriage. She tries to explain how deceived and how broken she really feels, but Don doesn't understand. In his eyes, he wasn't with another woman; he was only looking at images on a screen.

The reality of the situation is that pornography is a form of adultery, and just because millions of American men and women view it and pay billions for the vile material, doesn't erase the untold damage done to marriages. How can a woman compete with an airbrushed model who doesn't need emotional interaction? In the same way, men whose spouses view pornography feel equally inadequate to not only perform, but generate desire from their wives.

What are the consequences of pornography in marriage? Not only can the deception lead to a break in trust, but the offended spouse also feels cheated upon by their partner. Jesus said if a man looks upon a woman with lust, he has all ready committed adultery with her in his heart (Matthew 5:28). For the offended, it is just as if her partner has had an affair, which is the same self-defeating, gut-wrenching, dream-shattering, slap-in-the-face nightmare one would go through upon discovering a flesh-and-blood adulterous relationship. Regardless of whether or not it is ever discovered and confronted, it can wreak havoc on the intimacy in the marriage. Offenders who view pornography may find their wives less attractive and may lose their ability to become not only satisfied but even aroused by their less-than-perfect partners who are not willing to engage in the same kind of acts, respond as frequently as the offender would like, or meet the unreasonable demands compared to their fantasized rivals.

Research has shown that pornography creates a dopamine response in the brain, much like that of drugs. When the brain sees something new, something taboo, the hormonal and chemical release creates an adrenaline rush. Those who view pornography start by viewing nudity, but just as drugs lose their affect and as their bodies grow accustomed to them, they need more to satisfy the need. Soon, simple nudity is not enough, and the viewer needs to view harder material. The sense of taboo becomes satiated, and viewers eventually need perverse, possibly even pedophilic, material to create the same chemical response in the brain. If you do not believe me, look at the number of kidnappings and murders of innocent children involving sexual abuse. I understand that this is disturbing, but it is a direct result of the availability of pornography and the online use and proliferation of it, and we need to understand the connection with pornography, the cycle of addiction, and connection with pedophilia.

Kasey must confront her husband and explain the depth of her pain. Unless Don is willing to see the truth and acknowledge fully what he has done and actively overcome it, their marriage will suffer. There are situations such as these, where tough love is necessary. Couples must be in a relationship in which they are willing and able to hold each other accountable. Without this accountability and without the willingness of either party to listen or to own up to their issues, relationships cannot be healthy.

What do couples do when there has been a break in trust through infidelity, deception, or lies? Most of the time when a couple has encountered a break in trust, the offender wants the offended to forgive them and to move on quickly. For example, if a man has had an affair, he feels that he has apologized profusely, lived with her anger for long enough, and asks, "When will I ever be able to live this down?" The offender hates having to feel the sting of the offense over and over, reliving it every time they tell the story. Let's pretend Don, in our previous example, acknowledges that he has hurt Kasey and admits that his behavior has, in effect, been as though he had an affair. Don wonders, "When will I ever be forgiven? Will we ever be able to have a decent relationship where this doesn't affect us?" Many counselors will ask, "How long have you engaged in this adulterous behavior? If it happened over the course of a year, then you should give your wife at least a year to overcome this issue—*if* she is willing to forgive you.

It is truly amazing the lengths to which people will go to avoid owning and acknowledging the extent to which they have hurt others. People will justify their behavior, blame another spouse, and do whatever they can to place the emphasis elsewhere, trying to do everything possible to avoid responsibility for their actions. Maybe it is a form of self-preservation or is a defense mechanism, but in either case, until the offender owns his or her part in the problem completely, without making excuses, the healing process will be hindered. Offenders need to stop blaming, stop focusing on everyone else, and look inward. They need to see the extent of the harm they have caused and take time to show the offended person how much they have hurt them and prepare for the long road to recovery.

Offenders cannot expect the offended to have a complete recovery or put any other demands upon the offended. They must be patient, bear the resentment and emotions that the other partner will eventually experience, and be willing to communicate commitment in the middle of it. They must pray that God will open the offended person's eyes to see through the pain and realize their willingness to change. They must be completely transparent, make sure they deal openly and honestly, keep commitments, and allow the offended to see their consistency by catching them telling the truth, being on time, and following through with their promises. Offenders have no right to be resentful when the issue is discussed and should not put a time limit on the grieving process.

Marriage is like a three-legged stool with the legs of commitment, trust, and communication. Just as removing a leg of a three-legged stool will cause the person sitting on it to fall, couples need all three of these elements to feel secure and have a healthy foundation. Couples need to be assured of, experience, and develop commitment over time. While trust can be broken, bruised, and tattered, it can be repaired. Many trust issues exist within individuals before being married, and they need to be addressed honestly and adequately. These problems desperately need to be overcome to avoid isolation and promote the openness and honesty necessary to experience oneness in marriage. Couples cannot be healthy without good communication skills. Unless partners are willing to share, to understand, and to express their feelings, they will never be able to experience complete intimacy or overcome obstacles and resolve problems.

Being married means being willing to sacrifice. One of the greatest parallels of marriage and Christianity is the willingness to lay aside what we want, put aside the selfishness and the sense of entitlement we have and put our partner first. Society

THOMAS C. BATES, M.S.

teaches us that we deserve to have everything we want and to experience all the indulgences we desire and that marriage is a way to have all our needs met. In addition, society deems marriage as the end of the line with regard to happiness. Once two people are married, many feel that there is no more adventure to be had. Nothing could be further than the truth. Marriage is difficult, there are obstacles, and it does in part force us to examine our personality flaws and immaturity, but it is a beautiful union of souls. Marriage is one of the most magnificent pictures of God's ultimate command. Living with another person, accepting who they are, overlooking faults and making a relationship last every day is the epitome of love. Anyone who has been married for very long will tell you that if you have that selfish mindset, you will be constantly disappointed.

Marriage is not about my wants, my needs, and my desires but is putting my partner first, giving, sacrificing, and caring for another more than myself. Just as Christ laid down His life and bore the cross undeservingly, God calls us to die to ourselves, love our spouse, and do so without keeping score. First Corinthians 13 is often called the *love* chapter and says, "Love keeps no record of wrongs" (1 Corinthians 13:5). Marriage should not be one-sided, rather, it should involve a partnership in which both are willing to work together. At the same time, spouses ought not become the fairness police! As long as we are keeping score and placing the emphasis on another's actions, we will never be satisfied.

"Be kind and compassionate to one another, forgiving each other, just as in Christ God forgave you" (Ephesians 4:32).

God does not desire us to be doormats and to have a lopsided relationship in which we do all the work and our partner only takes from us. We are called to love ourselves in the ultimate command. So we should care enough about ourselves to expect our partners to love us. However, we must realize that selfishness is the vilest enemy and is the greatest barrier to a healthy marriage, and our expectations should be reasonable. I personally believe that overcoming selfishness is a life-long pursuit, and we never fully reach the pinnacle of unselfishness until we reach heaven. We can grow, and we can become less selfish and attain some measure of success with regard to putting others ahead of ourselves, but I believe it is a lesson which lasts throughout our lifetime.

There are many lessons to be learned with marriage. Beyond selfishness, another important aspect is learning that our partner cannot satisfy all our needs. Many people have searched for the perfect partner—one who will complete them. After three or four marriages, people (hopefully) come to realize that there is no perfect partner. Marriage in itself cannot create happiness and cannot create contentment. Satisfaction and happiness can only come through a healthy relationship with God; there is a void in our lives that only Christ can fill. Without a deep, meaningful relationship with Christ, people will always look for other ways to become complete. Until we come to the place in our lives where we realize nothing can fill our hearts but Christ, we will try to fill the emptiness with many things.

Relationships can very easily be confused with a recipe for happiness, and unfortunately it can lead to serious disappointment. Marriage will rarely, if ever, fulfill unmet needs, and as long as we have unhealthy expectations, we will never be satisfied in our marriages. When we have a healthy, daily heart-to-heart union with Christ that truly makes us complete, a marriage partner will be an added blessing rather than a source of dissatisfaction.

Finally, couples must take time to regularly be together and to talk without distractions. Partners must make consistent time to talk about issues, resolve problems creatively. More than anything else, couples need to continue dating and to keep the flame alive no matter how long they have been together, spending intimate time together. Making marriage work requires effort to keep it not only pure, but high on the list of priorities in life. A healthy marriage means happier children, better employment, and a joyful, more contented life. The ultimate commandment means loving our spouses completely, and other than our devotion to God there is no greater calling in life.

LEAVING A GREAT LEGACY

Parents need not leave a monument to themselves in this life. They do not need an accumulation of wealth to have a great impact on this world. Everyone dies, and none of us will take anything to heaven but our soul. The greatest thing parents can do is to pour their hearts into their children to disciple them and train them to be godly men and women. Above all else, what drives our parenting should be the goal of developing our child's character.

Leaving a legacy means that we are vigilant as parents to be teachers. Our focus should be ensuring that our children learn all they need to learn to be obedient to God, to other authority figures, and to recognize the enemy when they see him coming. Children are an instant source of accountability. I will never forget when I heard my then four-year-old daughter from the back seat of our van scream, "Get out of the way, you slow-poke!" to another car. I knew then I needed to be more careful with my words. They learn how to behave or misbehave and speak carefully or disrespectfully by watching us as parents. If you choose to make changes and lead by example, the accountability your children provide can be a great source of shaping your own character. The alternative, however, is that we can raise some, for a lack of a better clinical term, messed-up children if we do not take great care in training them properly.

Parents need a great deal of balance to manage all that accompanies parenting. We must not push them too much but help them develop a sense of excellence at the same time. We have to give them enough nurturing to help them feel loved but avoid coddling them so that they cannot function on their own. And we must remember that each of them is unique. We must take an individual approach to disciplining and shaping them according to their personality.

The youngest in a group of siblings is often one who struggles with responsibility and attention-seeking behavior. Our third daughter, Chloe, is a "mother hen," and we had to work hard to allow her to help but avoid doing everything for our youngest son, Gabriel. Gabriel never had to talk or ask for anything—our little over-achieving Chloe would get everything before he asked and would tie his shoes for him, brush his teeth, and pour his drinks before he could bat an eye. It has taken time to teach Chloe to help Gabriel learn on his own and still encourage that urge in her to serve others. In addition, we do not want our daughter to feel responsible to parent her younger brother, and we had to explain that she does not have to work all the time to please others.

We must be careful in our efforts to nurture our children. Give the children too much space, and you are neglecting them; hover and overprotect them, and they will never learn independence. Children who are overprotected and who never learn to make decisions on their own may wind up marrying controlling and possibly abusive spouses. Single mothers and even two-parent families may unintentionally teach their daughters to be so fiercely independent they often do not have room for a husband—let alone encourage him to lead. I have seen a pattern where, especially single mothers, teach their daughters to prepare for the eventuality of taking care of themselves. There is absolutely nothing wrong with that; all children need to learn to be self-supporting. But the problem arises when a son or daughter grows up so self-sufficient that they cannot be interdependent and cannot co-exist with a mate. Self-reliance and the ability to care for oneself should be balanced with a desire to submit to another and to make room for another person's disposition and personality. While I believe a man should be the servant-leader of the home, I believe he should heed his wife's intuition and make decisions in light of her valuable insight and discernment. Submission and equality must be modeled and taught to our children in our homes. Willingness to submit should be combined with an unwillingness to be controlled or dominated. Inner strength and boundaries must be mingled with gentleness and a desire for harmony. All these traits work together to create a healthy relationship.

Do you teach your children to share but still teach them to value their possessions and take care of them? Do you allow your children to have a few precious things that they do not have to share? One day, your child will be married, and he or she will need to be willing to share finances, time, and their life with another. At the same time, they need to value their possessions and finances in order to have what they need to survive. Money is not the root of all evil; rather, the love of it is what swings us out of balance (1 Timothy 6:10). Though it is not the most important part of life, money is important, and good stewards of God's resources take care of the possessions He has entrusted to them. These are the lessons your children need to learn. Unless you as a parent are making an effort to instill these values to help them cultivate and practice learning these skills, they will never learn them.

Have you inscribed one of the most valuable lessons of all into your children's hearts—the ability to say *no* when it is appropriate? Children need to learn proper boundaries and how to be able to say no without feeling guilty. Saying no comes easily for children who are strong-willed, but children who are people-pleasers need to be able to learn that difficult skill. If not, they will be in danger of being influenced by their peers and in danger of drug and alcohol abuse, promiscuous relationships, and other enticements.

One of the most powerful methods of discipline is the concept of giving your children choices. This is, I believe, the best approach in training your children out of all the tools available today. By "choices,"

I mean we give our children the choice of obeying us or experiencing consequences. "Mark, you can choose to turn off the game and come to supper, or you can choose to have no television before bedtime." This gives Mark an opportunity to do the right thing or give up something he wants. "Rebecca, you can choose to clean up your room properly or choose to surrender your cell phone for three days." Giving your children opportunities to choose obedience helps them feel a sense of power and control over their lives, but it also prepares them for adulthood. I may choose as an adult to get a job, or I may choose to be homeless.

With the concept of choices, your children will have a chance to practice learning obedience in a safe environment so that they are better able to make good decisions when it really counts. I want my children to learn to make good choices and experience consequences now, so they can choose to say no when someone who has been drinking asks them to jump in their car. This is very helpful for teenagers who are trying to learn independence feel as though they have power, but it can also help younger children, as well. Pick one behavior you are trying to correct at a time and focus on that for a week. Do not overuse this, but practice it week by week and see if it works. I have found it to be very helpful with my children.

What is the goal of parenting? Of course, we want to raise healthy children who become healthy adults. We want to develop their character. We must pick our battles carefully, focusing on matters of character rather than their inclinations or personality quirks. We must never discipline them from a standpoint of embarrassment. What others think about you as a parent is not nearly as important as instilling your values and ensuring your child's character is being shaped properly. With two children affected by autism, I can tell you I have endured many stares and many situations where other people have probably thought, *What a terrible parent. Look at that girl acting so crazy. Can't he make her shut up?*

I remember a story of an autistic child feeling uncomfortable in a crowded restaurant. The child was crying uncontrollably until the family finally decided to have their food packaged to take home and leave. As they got up to leave, the crowd in the restaurant erupted into applause. Can you imagine the frustration on the part of the parents? Do not always assume children are undisciplined. A child who cannot communicate cannot always express themselves appropriately. We discipline our daughter to the extent of her ability to understand, and I can assure you, for the most part that she is well-behaved. But there are times when she is very upset and has no other means of saying so except crying. Be patient with other parents—especially with those who have children with special needs.

If our goal is to help our children become functioning, healthy adults, how do we accomplish that? We must begin shaping their character early. "Train a child in the way he should go, and when he is old he will not turn from it" (Proverbs 22:6). That means we are charged with the duty of training our children. At the same time, the verse says "in the way he should go." According to the Hebrew translation, that means according to their bent. In other words, we do not need to force our children to go in the direction we want them to go with regard to their career, sports interests, or life goals. We need to be sensitive to their desires, their skills, gifts, and personalities and encourage them in that direction. We need to be flexible to that extent and use their God-given tendencies to help shape them.

If your child is interested in drama, find a place for him to flourish. Look for opportunities for him to serve within the church in puppet ministry or skits. Our oldest son is stocky—like me. While I played a year of college football, Jordan has absolutely no interest in sports. Often when we meet new people and they see the fact that my thirteen-year-old son looks like he is eighteen, they say, "You should be a linebacker!" Jordan loves writing skits, making movies, and all things drama. We have encouraged that in him. Jessica and I have endeavored to never push him toward anything he does not want to do. Find an interest inventory through your school counselor or online and help your child find that that interests him. All children need some sense of confidence and a sense of mastery in their lives. If a child feels gifted in an area and can begin pursuing it, they will make better grades and focus on that life goal, and I can assure you that it will make your life easier as a parent.

THOMAS C. BATES, M.S.

Having been a high school teacher, I can tell you children who have a life goal are much more motivated and make much better students than those who are filling a desk at school. More importantly, feeling a sense of mastery will give your child the confidence he or she needs to enjoy their youth and to develop a healthy identity and nurture positive feelings of self worth. To some who are reading this, it may sound like a bunch of psychological nonsense. But helping your child find success and helping identify and hone their gifts is invaluable. Confidence and self-worth are of utmost importance in helping your child find who they are in this world.

Teenagers are typically an exceptional challenge just by the very nature of their age. If you consider your teenage child to be a perfect angel who does everything she is told and never makes wrong decisions, please count your blessings. But at the same time, prepare yourself for the possibility of a Dr. Jekyll and Mr. Hyde transformation—perhaps even overnight. Hormones, lack of brain development, emotional peaks, and plunging valleys await. As one of my counselor friends put it, almost all teenagers could have a clinical diagnosis of bipolar disorder. A typical teenager could be in tears during breakfast and be laughing on the way to school. Teenagers and drama go hand in hand, and the slightest little turn of events can create an explosion of epic proportions. One of my most difficult challenges as a parent of a teen is in not being pulled into the vortex of his epic meltdowns. My blood pressure has been put to the test, and I am learning to keep a poker face while I witness these turbulent emotions.

In addition to the emotional roller coaster are the identity crisis and the gradual pulling away from mom and dad. Typically, developing teens begin challenging parental authority and want to test the boundaries. When parents say no to requests for more freedoms and place limits upon them, teenagers want to know why. This is absolutely normal, and one of the hardest parts of parenting teens is in teaching them to maintain respect and yet allowing them more freedom to question authority. While we as parents still have the right to throw down the "because I said so" gauntlet, we must understand the fact that authoritative parenting need not be authoritarian. We do not have to maintain a Hitler-*esque* authority structure. We can still raise children to have healthy respect for authority and learn to respect us as well as other adults without crushing their spirits.

As a former teacher and youth pastor, I have witnessed many teens who completely rebelled against their parents the moment they turned eighteen. Many teens choose to rebel even when they have perfect parents. However, often rebellious teens are a result of parents who were dictators, refusing to respect their children's right to express themselves in a healthy fashion. We must teach our children to respect authority and to learn anger management but give them room to grow and understand why we place limits upon them. There is a proper way to express oneself respectfully that does not appear insolent. Remember, healthy children are not robots who obey because they have to but rather because they love us and want to show it by doing what we say. Teaching your child to grow a spine and to be strong enough to avoid people and activities that would hurt them requires cultivating this healthy notion of questioning the world around them and knowing why rules are in place.

In addition, I have seen that the most dangerous teen is one whose parents have conflicting styles of authority. When dad lays down the law and mom contravenes what he said, the child has no sense of direction. The result is rebellion. Passive parents, or worse yet, *conflicting* parents create children with no discipline and no respect for authority. That is why many teachers are retiring today and many school systems are often helpless to work with American teenagers. The dynamic of divorced, guilt-ridden parents who create these conflicting parental styles has caused a major shift in the behavior of children today. Through the concept of co-parenting, divorced couples who share custody of children *must* work together to have a unified parenting style to create order for children of divorce.

One of the ways to discourage rebellion in adulthood is to develop a healthy bond with your child. Gary Chapman, in his book *The Five Love Languages for Children,* explores the need for maintaining this bond. Dr. Chapman discusses the importance of keeping your child's "love tank" full in order to ensure your child will respond properly to discipline. It is not enough to tell your child you love them, they must sense that they are loved. In doing so, Dr. Chapman expresses the need for finding your child's unique "love language." Once we understand how our child expresses love, we learn to speak their language and they can begin to feel loved. For example, if your child wants to show love to you and spends hours creating a gift for you that is special, chances are their love language is gift giving. Giving your child a special gift will make your child feel loved completely, and you will be speaking the language of love that they understand. If you witness your child expressing kind words to their sibling as a show of affection, chances are one of their love languages is words of affirmation. Your child will glow when you take your time to identify and specifically affirm them with something positive they have done.

More than any other part of parenting, ensuring your child knows that you love them is supreme. The ultimate command is our highest calling, and your children must not only experience love from you, but have it modeled by you as well. Teaching your children how to love is equally important. Many parents express conditional love; when their children are obedient, they receive rewards and adulation. Unfortunately, when these children disobey, they receive coldness, consequences, and sometimes rage from the very same parents. Children need to be made aware, regularly, that they are loved constantly—regardless of their behavior. Positive and

THOMAS C. BATES, M.S.

negative reinforcement are good tools, but parents need to make sure they convey love at all times—especially when children fail. I encourage you to take your child's face in your hands, whether they are two or fifty-two, get very close to them, and tell them unashamedly, "I love you, now, always, and forever, no matter where you go, no matter what you do."

Much more could be said regarding parenting beyond what could be contained in the pages of this book. But it is never too late to start, and you must make a concerted effort, no matter how confident you are as a parent, to grow. Discipline your children early and win the battle for authority while they are young. Consult a counselor, watch *Supernanny*, or do whatever you have to do to prepare yourself. Concentrate upon your child's character and begin to shape them as soon as they are able to understand. Dr. James Dobson, the founder of *Focus on the Family,* has many books that are invaluable resources. Always, you must pray continually for your children. Raising your children is serious business, and pouring your life into them is a sacred duty that is yours alone. May God keep you focused always—vigilant and competent to finish the task of raising your children. They are your ultimate legacy.

LOVING OUR CHURCH FAMILY

Why are so many leaving the church today? What is happening to the body of Christ and to the church in general? There are many possibilities that deserve consideration. Our schedules have become so busy and our lives so complicated that we have little time for anything other than life at home. Two-income families have so little time for housecleaning and errands and for the business of the family that they find it hard to work church into their schedules. Single parents struggle with this issue above all, and yet they need support from a loving congregation more than most. People have, in this busy generation, circled the wagons and placed most of their energies upon their family.

We have become very isolated in this electronic age, and social activities are dwindling with our ability to communicate through social media, instant messaging, and text messages. Others have grown weary with church, the traditionalism, and the tired, old way it has been done for hundreds of years. The church often places a lack of emphasis on youth, lacks the willingness to pay youth pastors, fund youth programs, or involve young people in the life of the church. This is a problem for some and can turn away many young families. Some have been burned by a congregation that left them out to dry, or abandoned them when they needed it most. Others have watched in horror while a congregation split over a pastor's affair, or some other public disgrace. Divisions over worship styles, leadership structure, or a decision to grow or stay small are sadly all too common.

Regardless, church is dwindling, and the world is suffering as a result. While society is turning inward, churches are trying to reach into homes and help them recognize the value of fellowship with other believers. Many churches are doing what they can to provide traditional worship services for those who enjoy rich, passionate hymns that provide not only pleasant memories of a happier time but are laden with practical, theological wisdom, as well. But congregations are also offering contemporary, heart-felt worship that seems to usher people into the very throne room of God. Both styles are wonderful, and both have significance with regard to helping people understand God better, worship Him more deeply, and experience Him abundantly.

Some churches are doing a marvelous job of providing drama for teens and allowing them to take part in not only the work of the church (ushering and receiving tithes and offerings) but participating in the worship service, as well. Yet many have continued to grow bitter toward churches. Among those disgruntled with church, some have experienced some type of affront from another in the congregation that has left a bad taste in their mouths toward any organized, spiritual endeavor. For those people who have been snubbed by another, openly wounded or silently left out, no amount of visitation, warmness or outpouring is capable of rebuilding their trust. What a travesty to think that the body of Christ, people who worship a God of love, could cause another to hate church! I imagine Satan loves those situations most when people who used to be faithful believers have a root of bitterness. It is heartbreaking to think the kingdom of God is being slandered, the church is being maligned, and society divided and conquered by those who used to be faithful Christians. What can we do to combat this trend?

God has called us to love, and the moment we forget this, the moment we place more emphasis on programs, activities, and events than building relationships, we forsake the opportunity to connect with others. In the creation story of Genesis, God saw everything He created as good with one exception. When He realized Adam was alone, He was displeased (Genesis 2:18). He created Eve so Adam could have a partner. God created man with a desire for intimacy and for fellowship with Him and with others. Church, if it is in fact modeled after Christ, should never lose sight of the desire to link one believer to another. We need fellowship, we need camaraderie, and we need to unite.

If we forsake this, we have given Satan the upper hand. But how do we do this successfully? How do we avoid allowing believers to say hello to one another on Sunday but never really get to know each other? We gravitate to this end, often desiring to worship God without connection because we do not want church members to know who we really are. If we can maintain these superficial, shallow relationships, we can avoid real discipleship, and we will not have one believer sharpen another, "...as iron sharpens iron" (Proverbs 27:17). How do we break through these barriers—these obstacles?

One method utilized in churches today is that of discipleship through small groups. Many pastors fear these groups because they are afraid that smaller groups will become factions, gossip mills that can create division in churches. But what was Jesus's method of reaching the world for Christ? He did not have a plan B. He poured His life into twelve men, one of whom defected, and they carried the gospel to the world. Paul commissioned Timothy to take what he had learned and entrust it to reliable men who would be qualified to teach others (2 Timothy 2:2). Discipleship is the ultimate way to not only teach others and improve their knowledge, but assist them in assimilating those truths to begin to incorporate them into their daily lives. Knowledge is critical in our spiritual lives, but wisdom is knowledge applied.

Why do physicians and counselors need an internship as part of their training? I would certainly shudder at the thought of a first-year intern performing surgery on me without a seasoned veteran his side! Why should Christianity be any different? There are many who profess Christ, but few who take it upon themselves to study the scripture to become mature believers without someone who can come alongside them and help them grow.

Discipleship helps the student *and* the teacher. As we disciple others, not only are we held accountable, but we also learn, too. As a teacher, my mathematics skills grew exponentially when I was faced with the myriad of questions by my students. In the same way, the process of teaching spiritual principles helps us better formulate them in our minds and understand better how to appropriate truth in life as we teach them to another.

One of the biggest problems in relating to others in the faith is the fact that we have so many differences, little idiosyncrasies, unique personalities, and diverse convictions about different aspects of the Christian life. Dissimilar tastes in music, theological views like eschatology and Calvinism and issues such as the consumption of tobacco or alcohol cause us to divide ourselves. When we walk into a large church, we (hopefully) see people from all walks of life, differing cultures, and backgrounds. Some are new to the faith, and others have been walking with God for years. Some are formal and closed in nature, others are open and easy to read, and others are somewhere in between. We ought to see blue collar and white collar people worshipping together. Recovering addicts with checkered pasts ought to be present, serving alongside those whose deepest sin was ripping off the tag from a mattress. Church should be a marvelous union of people who, regardless of backgrounds or personality, are able to work together, showing the world how to love and serve the way God commanded.

While some have the gift of compassion and grace, others have the gift of administration and have all the tenderness of a strand of barbed wire. It takes all kinds to make this world go around, and the same is true, to a certain extent, within the church. Problems exist, however, when one person, like spiritual sandpaper blurts out whatever is on their mind at the moment, wounding others. I find it very difficult to encounter those who are legalistic, quickly judge another, and do not take care when chiding another.

While God has called us to instruct each other and all of us need to be teachable and accountable to one another, we should do so carefully. The church is losing ground for many reasons, but it should not do so because some of its members refuse to have diplomacy and some measure of tactfulness with fellow believers. Love means, to the best of our ability, that we keep peace with one another. We need to work toward acceptance of brothers and sisters in Christ and look past differences of opinion and personality quirks and do what we can to help each other grow without bludgeoning each other in the process. While I am certainly not advocating for completely avoiding conflict or edifying the body of Christ, I think we could all learn to do so with a little more tact with the other believer in mind. Conflict is inevitable and important at times, but should be done with great care as discussed earlier.

One of the differences that stands out is the difference between those who have strayed far from God and those who have not. While, ultimately, God would have us be holy and we are commissioned by Him to pursue purity and holiness, human beings are inherently sinful. Why is it that some believers are able to walk a fine line and to keep their thoughts and actions pure while others seem to struggle? Why do we find that some believers, even famous characters from the Bible like David, stumble and fall after having done so much good? None of us is immune to the wiles of the devil, and he "...prowls around like a roaring lion looking for someone to devour" (1 Peter 5:8).

I have witnessed, in the lives of believers, the truth that those who have been forgiven much love much, and "...he who has been forgiven little loves little" (Luke 7:47). The truth of the matter is that there are no levels of sin, and God can use a murderer of Christians like Paul just as much as He can those who have been pure and not strayed from Him. There is no such thing as a person, other than Christ Himself, who is without sin. "All have sinned and fall short of the glory of God" (Romans 3:23).

The minute we begin pointing fingers and judging another, we are standing in judgment over them; and that is sin! God calls us to judge behavior, recognize sin, and even confront one another in love and do what we can to keep others from stumbling. But constructive, loving confrontation with the goal of restoring one another is very different from elevating ourselves by looking down upon another's failures. If I love my child, I will discipline him and confront him when he does something unsafe or unwise. But I do not berate him and belittle him in the process.

God desires for church members to unite and to become one. "If a house is divided against itself, that house cannot stand" (Mark 3:25). If every member of the church would have love as her or his goal, along with unity, compassion and grace, I believe we could win the world for Christ. Our purpose as believers is to model Christ and to leave the pleasing aroma of the love of God wherever we go whenever we encounter others. Our witness and our outreach should be a desire to attract others to Christianity. Does that mean we wear a mask and put on a happy face when we clearly do not feel cheerful? Of course not; we are real people with real problems. We encounter trials and face difficult situations, but we do so with the Holy Spirit inside us. We must allow God's grace, His mercy, and strength to make us strong when we are weak.

How many have been won to Christianity by witnessing a Christian enduring tragedy with assurance and confidence in spite of their pain? We are called to deal gently with one another and forgive each other just as we are forgiven. Above all, Christians should be the ideal model of working together and walking in unity. We must put aside petty differences, jealousy, strife, and contention, and live together in peace. The body of Christ is responsible for getting along with one another and proving to the world that even though we are unique individuals, we share a common goal of pursuing Christ and, most importantly, His love as we worship, interact, and grow together—working as a body should. Paul says, "If the whole body were an eye, where would the sense of hearing be? If the whole body were an ear, where would the sense of smell be?" (1 Corinthians 12:17).

If we are to truly love one another, we will put aside all favoritism. Pastors and members of churches should treat each person as a child of God. Why is it that Sunday, some feel, is the most segregated day of the week? I understand that people gravitate to churches within their own culture, but we must cross racial boundaries and cultural boundaries to truly be like Jesus. When He encountered the Samaritan at the well, the person most despised within the Jewish culture, He did not shrink back but interacted with her (John 4:7-26). We must stick together and look past the tattoos, dressing habits, sexual orientation, addiction, or any other issue that may be standing in the way of someone coming to Christ.

Yes, we have rules, by-laws, regulations that keep us as a church from disintegrating and becoming like the world. To the world, the church may ever appear as backward in our stance against evil. Our unyielding commitment to holiness, sexual purity, and separation from the humanistic worldview is often seen as weird by non-Christians. But in spite of our separation from the world we must, like Jesus, look past the exterior of others, look into the heart and do what we can to win them to Christianity. Our rules, by-laws, traditions, and pursuit of holiness should never be an excuse to exclude someone from being able to be loved, nurtured, taught, and moved forward toward belief in Christ. Yes, we must not become like the world or let it conform us, but rather hold to our convictions and stand against the tide of humanity. At the same time, we should be a beacon of hope and love to the world—not a place of exclusion, helping where we can to win everyone to the Lord.

I love what Rupertus Meldenius said in the early seventeenth century. "In essentials *unity*, in nonessentials *liberty*, in all things *charity*." Issues such as whether or not we believe in the virgin birth of Christ, a bodily resurrection, and Christ's gift of salvation as once for all, are essential tenets of our faith. But in issues such as the use of make-up, dresses for women versus pants, length of hair and other issues, we may disagree but still have the unity of faith. We will think differently and should be free to express our differences, but above all we must keep the bond of peace, stick together, and fight the real enemy rather than each other. We must have one body, one faith, one common goal of love: love for God and love for others. If the church can strive toward the ultimate command, we can overcome the enemy!

LOVING OUR COWORKERS AND FRIENDS

Many of us are surrounded by the greatest mission field imaginable—walking through the door every day in our place of employment. The challenge is often how to go about bearing the name of Christ without alienating yourself from coworkers. How can you avoid the jokes, maintain integrity, separate yourself from immorality, and interrelate with fellow employees at the same time? Accomplishing that balance can be the difference between being labeled as the office prude or feeling like a hypocrite. Many a Christian has found himself caught on the fence, longing to re-establish purity after having comprised their standards while relating to co-workers.

At this point, the inner struggle begins wondering, *What will they think of me now?* All the while, Satan plays their previous failures over and over in their minds. Will you be tossed back and forth by the waves of doubt and fear of what others think, or will you rise up and take a stand? Will you be ashamed of Christ, excuse yourself from being sanctified for fear of rocking the boat and risking promotions, advancement, or fitting in with the crowd at work? This is a time to focus more on your behavior and attitudes, while ignoring your fears of what others will think.

What are you willing to risk to be obedient to Christ's calling in your life? Will you shine your light in your workplace regardless of how dark it may be? Are you willing to find other believers and unite with them or remain in the shadows, hiding your Christianity for fear of scrutiny? Answer the call! You must be prepared, though, for the eventuality of persecution.

If your place of employment is cold toward God, you will more than likely have to endure being harassed or held up to the microscope by other employees. The only acceptable intolerance, often, is toward Christianity. The colder your workplace is, the darker the environment, the greater the need and the brighter your light will shine. Often, the harshest places, the rougher the unbeliever, the more ripe they are for the gospel. Always remember that when people forsake faith in Christ, they are not rejecting you but Christ *in* you. I recently talked with a person that we'll call John with whom I used to work who had become a Christian since that time. When we talked about a fellow employee, David, who was a Christian back then, John told me he couldn't stand David and that he "hated his guts." Looking back, he said he realized it was God inside David that conflicted with John. John said he knows now that it was David's spirit that disgusted him, and the devil inside John wanted no part of David. When people are unbelievers, their human nature and even the enemy does whatever it can to keep them away from Christians. That is what we are fighting against when we want to win others to Christ.

The best way to persuade others and to build relationships with them is to, as much as possible, avoid confrontation. There may be a time and a place for that, but you must ensure you have a strong relationship with them before doing so. Humility, without a trace of pride or boastfulness, is much more effective than bludgeoning someone with the gospel and having an antagonistic attitude. It makes sense that a know-it-all attitude is the quickest way to alienate yourself from those with whom you work. Offering ideas and suggestions does not have to include the need to downplay another's ideas as inferior. Listening to others, validating their opinion, and showing respect is the best way to express the love of Christ. Having a humble, loving attitude, avoiding pushiness or the need to dominate conversations is the healthiest way to illustrate Christ's love.

On the other hand, humility does not mean you have to be a doormat. I have worked with supervisors and owners who, knowing I was a Christian, were prone to take out their frustrations on me knowing that I was a perfect target—one who wouldn't retaliate. There are times when we must not only stand our ground morally with regard to ethical principles but stand up for ourselves personally. Meekness does not mean wimpyness. We must learn to walk the fine line between compromise and prudishness and meekness and humility without being a pushover.

How can we win our workplace for Christ? The secret is to build upon the strengths we have and to find fellow Christians in our workplace. Inevitably, we will find ourselves in an environment where the only other believers are from a different background, denomination, or conflicting belief system. You could find, for example, that the only other person(s) of faith are people who are Catholic or Jewish, and you are from a Presbyterian background. *How am I to build an alliance with them when our faith is so different?* you may wonder. What do you have in common? You all agree upon faith in God, and while this may not be a perfect blend, you may still be able to pray together, and if nothing else, build relationships with them.

As much as you are able, find other believers whenever you can. If you can find persons with similar faiths, even if there are a few differences you will be able to find strength in unity. Build upon common ground and avoid allowing your petty differences to divide you. Meet for prayer or breakfast and start a Bible study or a book study at work. Be prepared for disagreements and set ground rules so your debating won't keep you from productive growth. Keep working toward alignment, focusing on the essentials upon which you agree.

Respect, genuine concern, and compassion can go a long way in the workplace. Offer to pray for nonbelievers and listen to their struggles and take note of sicknesses, possible promotions, and even the health of the business itself. All of these can be building blocks—bridges between yourself and those without faith. Building relationships is the most powerful tool in winning the world for Christ.

In this economy, many struggle with fear of losing one's job. It is hard to think about standing up for Christ, when you are doing all you can do to survive. Selling out a little, to keep food on the table, is a necessary evil in the eyes of some. It is a difficult situation to find oneself in a job where ethical principles, living with integrity, would mean losing business and being unable to compete in this hostile market. Many have contemplated quitting for years only to find they are afraid of starting over at their age and losing the security of the job they have had for years. Many are miserable and are longing for a way out. Sometimes a leap of faith is exactly what God has in mind; other times God's answer is to stay right where you are. Obviously, the best policy is to have another job lined up before quitting, but sometimes God will ask you to do something that requires great faith. I would certainly recommend bathing every decision in deep prayer and seeking a multitude of counselors whom you trust before leaving a job. Regardless, God wants to use you, today—right where you are—to win non-believers to Christ in your workplace.

Friends outside of work are a source of ministry, as well. But many of the same rules apply with regard to aligning oneself with people across denominational boundaries and seeking unity. Finding balance between compromise and over-sanctification is crucial. Cocooning oneself with only Christian friends can make you just as ineffective as surrounding yourself

THOMAS C. BATES, M.S.

with non-Christian friends and behaving as they do. All of us need an inner circle, a group of trusted individuals who can bear our burdens, to keep us accountable and sharpen us. True friends are there when you need them but are also willing to call you out when you need it. We ought to be very careful however, with friends who are non-Christians. While we should reach out and build relationships with unbelievers, we need to be sure that we are not allowing ourselves to conform to an unbelieving world. We become like the people with whom we spend time. I often use an example to illustrate the principle of conformity. How many know of a teenager who leaves for college and comes home for the holidays? Have you ever noticed the way they talk when they come home and how, at times they seem to speak and carry themselves like a totally different person? Adults are not much different. We pick up the same habits, and the people with whom we surround ourselves *do* rub off on us. I pray you have a large, diverse group of friends but that you pick them carefully and take great care in making sure your closest companions are spiritually beneficial rather than anchors that drag you into the mire of complacency, conformity, and mediocrity.

LOVING OUR NEIGHBOR

There is a wonderful ministry through the Mission America Coalition, a part of the Lighthouse Movement, called "Loving Our Communities to Christ." This ministry is focused on winning America to Christ one community at a time. There are other ministries focused on providing hospitality to one's neighbors, building relationships with them to minister to them and encourage them toward faith in Christ.

The idea is to focus on making friends with your neighbors and making yourself available to them. Inviting them to dinner, sometimes just offering to help them in some way can lead them to faith. Many of us could do a better job of being a good neighbor. In this day and age, most do not even know their neighbors, and many prefer it that way. It is sad to think there are many lonely people, who are depressed, isolated, and longing for friendship while Christians are living right down the street and will never have an opportunity to know Christ. These people may never experience the acceptance, love, and fellowship that could be theirs as a believer. Will you reach out and take some time once a week or once a month to make friends with your neighbors?

Our busy lives have become so isolated and so inundated with technology and "hermit-like" living that we rarely go outside—let alone speak to people next door to us. I have recognized a trend that seems evident; the closer one lives to neighbors, the more isolated, less social, and less apt they are to be open and friendly. The more crowded the environment, the less likely people are to be neighborly. Ironic, isn't it? God created us to interact with others, and while we can keep up with others through social media outlets, face-to-face interaction is the only way to truly connect with others. I pray you will make an effort to be social.

While many of us are very busy, all of us could do a better job of reaching out. In my family, as with other families with special needs children, we have very little time for social activities. Finding a regular baby-sitter is rare when specialized care is needed for your children. My wife and I used to go out on dates every four to six months, and as a counselor that is a hard thing to admit. Fortunately, we have found a respite service where local churches rotate one week per month watching special needs children and their siblings. We have been able to have an actual date for over two hours, and it has been wonderful. Social activities are scarce, as we have so much extra work cleaning and attending to our children's needs. But all of us need to do what we can to focus on being a better neighbor—on winning our community for

Christ. Life is not meant to be lived alone, and we must do what we can to advocate for maintaining a social society. Set a goal of interacting with others once a week. Get in touch with your neighbors and make time to get to know them, today.

LOVING THE UNLOVABLE

Having traveled across the nation as a truck driver, I have experienced a variety of cultural distinctions within this great nation of ours. Growing up in rural Alabama, I was isolated, and my experience with regard to cultural diversity was limited. In my travels, I found that while there are cultural differences that exist in different regions of our country, some things are the same. And unfortunately I was surprised to find that many of the negative aspects, like bigotry and racism, exist as much in the Northeast as in the deep South, and virtually everywhere else.

I was fortunate to have a mother who taught me to love regardless of the color of a person's skin. My mother grew up in rural Alabama and was raised to treat African Americans as second-class citizens. She recounted to me, with disgust, stories of being scolded for waving to an African American child or of watching her father "blessing out" an African American man who had the audacity to knock on her family's front door rather than go around to the back. Needless to say, my mother was adamantly opposed to this and endeavored to raise me differently.

Since that time, I have developed a deep conviction to build relationships across racial boundaries and advocate for racial reconciliation. I have African American friends who tell me stories of being raised to hate white people, and God's love and scripture teaching them differently.

I will never forget encountering two young men who, upon seeing my Christian T-shirt, asked my opinion of an inter-racial couple sitting nearby. They explained to me, after showing me their red bandanas in their back pockets, that they were in the Ku Klux Klan, and stated, "That's against the Bible, 'ain't' it?" I was dumbfounded and ashamed as I often am when encountering bigotry within not only my race but persons who perpetuate the stereotype that all southerners, specifically white Alabamians, are racist. I then proceeded to tell them the story of Miriam, Moses's sister-in-law, whom God turned leprous when she continued to gossip about Moses's Cushite (dark-skinned and presumably Ethiopian) wife. They had nothing to say, and I walked away sad, hoping God would change their callous hearts.

God shows no favoritism; He sees the heart. He saw David's inner worth when the prophet Samuel did not believe he was worthy as king (1 Samuel 16:6-13). God loves us in spite of our failures, utter sinfulness, and helplessness. His son bled and died for us. Prone to failure, weakness, addictions, pride, selfishness, lying, and cheating, we are not worthy of His love. How then can we look down on anyone? How dare we do so!

THOMAS C. BATES, M.S.

Do you show favoritism or do you love everyone equally? Do you stand up for the rights of others, or do you find yourself looking down on the weak? How do you feel about homeless people who choose to stay homeless or women who refuse to leave their abusive husbands and who keep their children in harm's way? The Latino mother who finds a way to be on welfare, to receive healthcare without citizenship, the mother who beats her children, or the father who beats his wife? Can you love a pedophile, a homosexual who has no desire to change, or a drug addict who has been in and out of rehab for the fifth time? Will you love them? God loves us, and we are unworthy. Will you refuse to love the unlovable?

Of course, I am not saying that we agree with the sinful lifestyles of others or that we accept that behavior. But we are called to love and to do what we can to help those who are without Christ find God. What kind of Christian are we if we do not love? We must stand against bigotry, model the love of Christ, and show the world what it means to be a true believer and to be patient with those who make mistakes. While we stand against sin and while we prevent the world from taking away our right to have convictions, we need to be filled with love for everyone—not just those who will love us back. It is easy to love those who love us. Real love is loving those who do not deserve it—those who, like us, deserve to be punished.

Will you build relationships across racial boundaries? Will you rise up against hatred and stand for those who are weak? Or will you look down in self-righteous indignation and judge them, knowing all the while we have weaknesses and frailties ourselves. All of us have had racism on either side of the racial boundaries poured into us over the years. It is up to us to break the cycle. Like Tony Evans said, "When you are in a war, you don't care what color the person is beside you as long as they are wearing the same uniform and shooting at the same enemy."

We must stand together, love each other, and stamp out hatred of all kinds. We can do it by loving one person at a time. Yes, teach your children convictions and keep the world from cramming its beliefs down their throats, but all the while teach them to love and teach them to express the same grace God gave us to others. Most of all, we must model that love in our own lives in how we relate to others. We can make a difference, and we must keep trying so that eventually racism will be all but extinguished. Love knows no bounds, it keeps no record of wrongs, it always protects, it always hopes, and it always perseveres (1 Corinthians 13:5, 7). Believe with me today that we can, through perseverance and hope in Christ, teach the world to love.

FORGIVING—LOVING THOSE WHO HURT US

"What difference does forgiveness make?" you may ask. "Why should I forgive?"

> Jesus said "Therefore, if you are offering your gift at the altar and there remember that your brother has something against you, leave your gift there in front of the altar. First go and be reconciled to your brother; then come and offer your gift. (Matthew 5:23)

First, God desires forgiveness. It is not a question of whether we want to or the person who hurt us deserves it, it is a matter of obedience. Second, forgiveness brings with it a release and a removal of the shackles we place upon ourselves by refusing to forgive. Aren't you glad God does not have the same view of forgiveness—the same weights and measures for mercy that we have?

If God held a grudge like me for one of my billions of sins, just one, I would never see the light of day again. I would be locked away forever.

Julia remembers the pain she suffered as a child, the way her father used to come home intoxicated and become enraged. Still fresh in her mind, she feels the sting of his belt, his fists over and over again in her head. When she finally left home, went to college and got married she thought she would be free from it. Unfortunately, she still struggles with trusting her husband, is constantly afraid that he will begin drinking, and her thoughts plague her relentlessly. Her father has quit drinking, but has never really acknowledged what he did to Julie, her mother or her sister. "How can I forgive what he did," she wonders, "when he never admitted it in the first place?" She knows forgiving him will help, but he has never learned from his mistakes; he is still the bitter, lonely old man he has always been.

Julie finds the courage, through relationships with friends at church, to go and see him. She brings him a picture of her children, and talks with him for over an hour. He admits the fact that he wasn't the greatest father in the world, but never really comes to the point of identifying his mistakes or asking forgiveness for what he has done. Julie has a decision to make, should she continue trying to reconcile, completely forgive him or not? Julie must realize it is not the offender, but we who suffer and are eaten away internally when we hold on to the hurt. She must do what she can to work through the situation. Julie must make a conscious decision on her part to forgive her father to experience healing, regardless of his repentance.

Forgiveness should be a process. It need not be something that is done quickly, on the surface. Saying the words "I forgive him" in your head, even out loud, is not enough. True forgiveness is choosing to release someone from the penalty of guilt, the debt that is owed, for the damage done to you. It must involve releasing that person, remembering your forgiveness when the thoughts creep into your mind again. Real forgiveness should take time. If you are truly willing to forgive, it should not depend upon some prescribed method, a series of demands, upon the person who hurt you. Forgiveness is an act of your will and takes place in your heart and your mind; it need not even involve the person who offended you.

If you want to attain closure, you might involve the offender. Maybe you need to go and see the person and explain that which you are forgiving in detail. Maybe you need to visit a grave or write a letter. In some cases, God will ask you to restore the relationship in spite of how difficult it may be. In other situations, it is in your best interest for the sake of safety or maintaining healthy boundaries to stay away from that person. The important part is to follow God's direction and be willing to be obedient regardless of your feelings. You can trust God to lead you to do what will be best in terms of healing your heart. I have worked with clients engaging in therapy in which the counselor plays the offender or the client pretends to speak to the person who hurt them in an empty chair. There are many ways to release the anger, attain some measure of closure, and process your feelings. Ultimately, forgiveness exists within you and resides with only you.

Maybe you are waiting for the offender to confess and learn from their mistake(s). Maybe you are refusing to forgive them because the person has not bothered to acknowledge what they have done. What you must realize is that you are not responsible for another's behavior. You do not have to answer for someone else's sins. You are accountable for your behavior—it is your thoughts, your reaction, and your part in this situation for which you are responsible. You alone will give account for how you respond to what has been done to you. As long as you are focused on the injustice, and continue to nurse the wound, you will remain in this self-made prison of pain and self-pity. Do you want out? Forgiveness is the key to unlocking the dungeon.

Do they deserve forgiveness? Not always. They, like us, will stand before God to account for their sins just as we will. There is one lawgiver and judge, one being worthy of standing in judgment over the inhabitants of this earth, and we are not Him (James 4:12). But we must realize that as long as we hold them in contempt, we are the imprisoned. Again, there needs to be a clear distinction between the act of forgiveness and doing what is necessary to process your feelings to move through stages of grief. These concepts should be separated, and I will refer to them as the act of forgiveness and processing your emotions.

Forgiveness does not mean we go through the motions of saying, "I forgive him," and it is over. Sometimes forgiveness takes years to experience fully. Dealing with and processing our emotions can often take years to get through. Why do I separate them?

Forgiveness is an act of the will, according to God's Word, and it is not an option. Matthew 5:14-15 says that if we forgive our brother, God forgives us. If we do not, He will not forgive our sins. While forgiveness is something we are required to do, processing our feelings, releasing the anger, is not mandatory. I can forgive someone but still choose to hold on to the anger. I can choose to forgive a person but still experience feelings of resentment every time I think about that person. Whether you choose to think of the two concepts as different or one in the same, when someone has been hurt deeply, the process of forgiveness, along with the emotions that accompany it, takes time.

When I truly forgive someone, I will still experience thoughts about what they did to me. It is in those moments of remembering that we either choose to remind ourselves that they are forgiven or allow the anger and resentment to smolder. Anyone who has experienced the betrayal of someone close to them or has been abused, taken advantage of, or otherwise deeply wounded will tell you that those feelings resurface over time. Perhaps there are people who are delivered from these wounds and attain complete release from these feelings immediately and permanently, but there are many others who do not. Wounds that are deep require attention, and a gradual healing often takes place.

I will never forget having been falsely accused and having my integrity called into question. I will never forget sitting in that court room, summoned there by someone who hated my guts. I remember being forced to sit in an adjacent room and listen to them spout lies about me for hours only to be denied the opportunity to defend myself. There are many other injustices with that situation I will not disclose. But for me, forgiveness was a process. Years later, I still have to remind myself that person is forgiven. The feelings, the emotions, and the need for having someone validate my feelings were important parts of the process.

When I was a young adult, I worked for a trucking company as a billing clerk, entering information for the Bills of Lading on items being shipped into the computer system. In addition, I worked loading trucks on the docks. The main secretary was responsible for auditing my work on the computer. For some reason unbeknownst to me, she apparently did not like me. She was not only surly and said unkind things but would specifically go out of her way to bring my mistakes, typos, and clerical errors to the terminal manager, even though auditing my work did not require her to do so.

It seemed as though she had it in for me, as though she wanted me to hear her going into the manager's office while she recounted my mistakes. At one point, she came to me and said, "I don't think you are cut out for this job. You don't seem to be able to do it."

Over time, I had built up frustration toward her, and I felt as though she scrutinized my every move. The pressure she put on me was so intense that I snapped. "I am working on a bachelor's degree in business, I type seventy words per minute, and I don't make many mistakes!" I yelled while storming out to the dock to take out my frustration. I went home fuming and spent many hours praying about the situation.

During my prayer time, God seemed to be impressing on my heart to love this woman. "How am I supposed to love her when she is so mean to me?" I asked. God kept at it, and I felt His inescapable nagging for me to forgive. God wanted me to love her, and I felt as though He wanted me to do so by going out of my way to genuinely show kindness, gentleness, and most importantly, respect. I cannot express how difficult it was to be respectful to someone who had no respect for me.

Over time, this woman seemed to soften and even invited me out to lunch a few times. I was able to not only build a relationship with her but was also able to share the love of Christ and what He had been doing in my life over time.

A few months later, I experienced a miracle. While some workers were doing plumbing work under my mobile home, the grass caught fire, and my mobile home was destroyed. I lost all of my clothing but was thankful that the volunteer fire department saved my pictures. Here is the miracle—this precious lady, a person whom I would have never guessed would do so, took me to the mall and bought me an entire new wardrobe! The very same person who seemed to despise me showed me such a kindness. God has an amazing way of turning things around.

I realize this kind of happy ending is rarely the case. The people God asks us to forgive do not always change, and many of them never acknowledge what they have done. There are many injustices in this life, and we seldom see the offender brought to justice. The point is that we are called to take the high road and to forgive, regardless of whether or not the offender comes clean. Forgiveness is about obedience. Forgiveness is about learning to see with the eyes of Christ and to understand what it means to experience injustice and to respond the way God has toward us. Will you choose to forgive?

Loving those who hurt us is fulfilling the ultimate command. Jesus showed us the greatest example of reconciliation, forgiving even those who drove the nails into his flesh and providing forgiveness and restoration through that sacrifice. How much more should we forgive those who hurt us? There are opportunities to confront those who hurt us at times and to express our frustrations. But God is in charge of justice, and He knows every tear we shed, every detail of our lives. Trust God and the infinite plan He has made just for you, be an agent of peace wherever you go. Live and fulfill God's high calling to love, and make it the basis for everything you do. Make love the theme of your life, influencing your thoughts, your attitude, and deepening every relationship. You will never be disappointed for fulfilling this ultimate calling.

BIBLIOGRAPHY

Cloud, Henry. *Changes That Heal*. Grand Rapids: Zondervan Publishing House, 1992.

Maslow, Abraham. *Motivation and Personality Second Edition*. New York, N.Y.: Harper & Row Publishing Inc., 1970.

Ortwein, Mary. *IDEALS of Kentucky*, "Mastering the Mysteries of Love." Last modified 6-14-11. Accessed December 15, 2011. http://www.skillswork.org/mml -curriculum/mastering-the-mysteries-of-love/

Stoner, Don. *Science Speaks: Online Edition*. Chicago: Moody Press, 2002. http://sciencespeaks.net/ (accessed June 14, 2011).

Swindoll, Charles. Good Reads, "Quotes." Last modified 2011. Accessed December 14, 2011. http://www.goodreads.com/author/quotes/5139. Charles_R_Swindoll.

Tolkien, J.R.R. *The Two Towers*. Boston: Houghton Mifflin Company, 1993.

ENDNOTES

1   Maslow, Abraham. Motivation and Personality Second Edition. New York, N.Y.: Harper & Row Publishing Inc., 1970.

2   Don Stoner, *Science Speaks: Online Edition*, (Chicago: Moody Press, 2002)http://sciencespeaks.net/ (accessed June 14, 2011), chap. 2.

3   Henry Cloud, *Changes That Heal*, (Grand Rapids: Zondervan Publishing House, 1992), 172-177.

4   J.R.R. Tolkien, *The Two Towers*, (Boston: Houghton Mifflin Company, 1993), 120.

5   Swindoll, Charles. Good Reads, "Quotes." Last modified 2011. Accessed December 14, 2011. http://www.goodreads.com/author/quotes/5139. Charles_R_Swindoll.

6   Ortwein, Mary. IDEALS of Kentucky, "Mastering the Mysteries of Love." Last modified 6-14-11. Accessed December 15, 2011. http://www.skillswork.org/mml-curriculum/mastering-the-mysteries-of-love/